*Real Estate Taxes and
Urban Housing*

REAL ESTATE TAXES
AND
URBAN HOUSING

JAMES HEILBRUN

COLUMBIA UNIVERSITY PRESS

New York and London

1966

James Heilbrun is Assistant Professor of Economics at Columbia University.

For A. G.

ACKNOWLEDGMENTS

I wish to express my gratitude to the Committee on Urban Economics of Resources for the Future, Inc., whose generous fellowship grant made it possible for me to begin this study with a year of full-time research and writing.

My wife lent indispensable support, not least by typing successive drafts from a Chinese puzzle of manuscript which certainly would have defeated anyone less patient and resourceful. That I owe much to Ernest M. Fisher, who first introduced me to the study of the housing market, is, I hope, apparent in the text that follows. I benefited greatly from the comments and suggestions of the members of the Public Finance Workshop at Columbia University, who read portions of an earlier draft of the work in 1960–61 and 1961–62.

It is, above all, a pleasure to record my very large debt to Professor Carl S. Shoup, who watched over this project cheerfully from start to finish. He and Professor William S. Vickrey, to whom I am also greatly indebted, gave their time freely and promptly and offered constructive suggestions far too numerous to catalog here. For the remaining errors and eccentricities I, of course, assume full responsibility.

JAMES HEILBRUN

New York
December, 1965

CONTENTS

Real Estate Taxes and
Urban Housing

CHAPTER ONE

INTRODUCTION

Urban housing policy in the United States underwent an important change in the early 1950s. The provision of standard housing for all city-dwellers remained its first objective, but new means were to be employed in the drive toward that disappointingly elusive goal. Without completely abandoning the older method of outright slum clearance coupled with new construction, we now began to experiment with novel ways of fostering the maintenance and rehabilitation of existing buildings. The new approach to the problem of urban slums has encouraged and has been encouraged by fresh attempts to bring economic analysis to bear on the subject. Thus far, however, there has been almost no discussion of the impact of real estate taxes on housing maintenance and rehabilitation. Although precise figures are not available, the best estimates are that real estate taxes take between 16 and 20 percent of the gross rent receipts of all rental housing. (See Table 1.1.) It is hardly possible that these charges, levied year after year, have only negligible effects on rental housing. Yet the question, important as it is for current urban housing policy, has never been analyzed with much care.

Perhaps economists have taken it for granted that our cities, faced with a rising demand for expenditures and with a narrow range of tax choices open to them, would never consent to significant changes in the real estate tax, so that it would be useless to examine the tax's impact on housing. Such acquiescence in institutional fate, however, leaves us with a typically American paradox: the federal (and even the state and city) government contrives subsidies to stimulate the improvement

TABLE 1.1

*Estimates of the Ratio of Tax Payments
to the Gross Rent of Housing*

	All U.S. rental housing[a]		
	1929	1939	1952
Gross space rent, $ billion	4.39	3.89	8.04
Property taxes, $ billion	0.84	0.87	1.68
Taxes as percent of rent	19	22	21

	New York City sample[b]		
	1925–29	1935–39	1950
Taxes as percent of gross income (all residential buildings)	15	22	17

	All U.S. nonfarm housing[c]
	1957
Personal consumption expenditure for private nonfarm housing, $ billion	32.028
Estimated property tax payments, $ billion	5.195
Taxes as percent of expenditures	16.22

[a] U.S. Department of Commerce, Office of Business Economics, as published in H. D. Osborne, "Rental Income and Outlay in the United States, 1929–52," *Survey of Current Business,* June, 1953, Tables 2 and 3, pp. 20–21.

[b] Leo Grebler, *Experience in Urban Real Estate Investment* (New York, Columbia University Press, 1955) Table 59, p. 254. Included as "Taxes" are negligible amounts of workmen's compensation and Social Security payments.

[c] Dick Netzer, *Economics of the Property Tax* (Washington, D.C., The Brookings Institution, 1966), Table 2–7, p. 29.

of housing, while the city takes in housing taxation as much revenue as it decently can. The literature itself reflects the paradox: one set of analysts is pleased to announce that property tax revenues since 1945 have grown with an entirely unexpected vigor, while another set busy themselves studying the various techniques by which the public can subsidize urban housing and renewal.

The present study is written in the belief that it is not useless to examine the impact of taxes on urban rental housing. On the contrary, it starts from the assumption that we ought to find out whether our traditional tax on the assessed value of real estate is compatible with the new emphasis on housing maintenance and rehabilitation and, if it is not, whether any feasible alternative method of taxing real estate is likely to be preferable. Before outlining the plan of the present study, however, it will be useful to sketch briefly the changes in American housing policy that led the author to undertake it.

In the 1930s, when the federal government took up in earnest the problem of housing the urban poor, "slum clearance" and public housing were made the foundation of national policy. Rightly or wrongly, urban slums had long been regarded as a prominent source of evil, and the New Deal was prepared to attack the evil at its roots. Slum clearance looked like a straightforward solution: simply knock down the worst blocks and replace them with subsidized public housing.

With the passage of the U.S. Housing Act of 1937, this prescription became national policy. It operated by what is now known as the "bulldozer" method: whole blocks of slums were razed and replaced by new publicly owned housing. The bulldozer method was acceptable during the 1930s for several reasons. First, there was apparently a substantial supply of vacant slum housing in most cities, so that razing slums on a modest scale did not significantly narrow the range of housing choices for the poor.[1] Second, the expenditure needed to build new public housing units was the sort of economic stimulant called for by President Roosevelt's pump-priming policy. Third, city planning was still design-oriented, was preoccupied, that is, with the physical aspect of the urban environment. Hence, the physical removal of slums was accorded a high priority.

World War II, however, radically changed the circumstances in which urban housing policy operated. Far from having an excess supply of slums, most cities after the war faced severe housing shortages.[2] As a result, "relocation" of uprooted tenants became a major problem for urban renewal authorities. Instead of seeking acceptable ways to spend money, the federal government, once reconversion was out of the way, was under pressure to minimize inflation by holding expenditures down. At the same time, students of urban housing and planning were increasingly aware of the shortcomings of pure and simple slum

[1] See data in Appendix A, Table A.1.
[2] See data in Appendix A, Table A.2.

clearance as a solution to the problem of substandard housing.
The bulldozer, they discovered, often destroyed viable social
structures along with decrepit physical ones. Blight, they em-
phasized, could not be halted once and for all by razing slums,
for it reappeared continually as neighborhoods aged and
changed. Housing and planning experts therefore began to ask
for a larger, more diversified kit of tools, out of which they
would be able to select the appropriate one for each part of
the job.

After the war these forces gradually worked a shift in the
direction of public policy. The bulldozer was not discarded
outright, but the search began for more discriminating methods
of urban renewal. The idea of "rehabilitation" began to take
hold, for it appeared that rehabilitation might successfully raise
housing standards without the physical, social, and aesthetic
dislocation that were thought to accompany massive public housing projects. Moreover, rehabilitation might be cheaper than
total clearance combined with total reconstruction and would
be "free," from a public point of view, if private owners could
be encouraged to undertake it on their own account.

Federal policy toward the problem of urban slums began
moving away from the pattern that had been established in
the 1930s when the Housing Act of 1949, under its now famous
Title I, provided federal assistance for slum clearance that
would be followed by private rather than by public redevelopment. Despite the new emphasis on private redevelopment,
however, the bulldozer was still relied upon to prepare the
ground. But the Housing Act of 1954 widened the breach with
the past. The federal government now encouraged localities to
develop comprehensive urban renewal plans that included
measures to stop the spread of blight and stimulate rehabilitation as well as to clear slums by the older techniques.[3]

___

[3] For a useful historical summary of federal housing legislation, see Martin
Meyerson, Barbara Terrett, and William L. C. Wheaton, *Housing, People, and
Cities* (New York, McGraw-Hill, 1962), Chap. 13. The historical development of
local housing policy and its relation to federal legislation is surveyed in Chap.
16 of the same volume.

The new interest in rehabilitation is visible both in publicly sponsored projects and in privately organized activity. An important example of publicly organized effort going forward under provisions of recent legislation is New York City's West Side Urban Renewal Area. This plan provides for the comprehensive renewal of a 20-block area on Manhattan's West Side. It is described by New York's City Planning Commission as

the first large scale effort to renew an entire neighborhood, utilizing in a coordinated fashion the many tools and techniques of housing and renewal made available over the years. . . . The Plan provides for redevelopment, rehabilitation and conservation as part of an appropriate neighborhood plan.[4]

An example of privately organized interest in rehabilitation is the work of ACTION, Inc. Established in 1954 as a direct result of a recommendation by President Eisenhower's Advisory Committee on Housing, ACTION describes itself as

the national, private, public service organization dedicated to fostering and supporting, on both local and national levels, organized citizen effort to create and maintain the best possible environment in our nation's cities. . . . Since its inception, ACTION's primary effort has been to mobilize public opinion in support of vigorous action to eliminate slums, rehabilitate and conserve neighborhoods, and stimulate urban renewal.[5]

Among ACTION's numerous programs, that of greatest interest to students of housing is a research project the results of which were published as the eight-volume ACTION Series in Housing

---

[4] City of New York, *Report of the City Planning Commission on the West Side Urban Renewal Area Final Plan*, May 29, 1962, p. 10. The Board of Estimate approved the final plan on June 26, 1962, and work began before the end of that year. See also J. Clarence Davics, III, *Neighborhood Groups and Urban Renewal* (New York, Columbia University Press, 1966), Chap. V.

[5] Quotation from *Fact Sheet*, August, 1962, a public information statement issued by ACTION, Inc., 2 West 46th Street, New York 36, N.Y. When founded in 1954, the organization bore the official name "The American Council to Improve Our Neighborhoods." The name was formally changed to ACTION, Inc., in 1959 and to Urban America–ACTION Council for Better Cities in December, 1965.

and Community Development. One of these volumes was devoted exclusively to the question of housing rehabilitation.[6]

Both private and public effort today seek to encourage the private maintenance and rehabilitation of existing urban rental housing. It is therefore entirely appropriate to ask does the traditional ad valorem real estate tax help or hinder these private activities? There are many ways of taxing real estate besides the traditional American method, and some of these have been used elsewhere. Are any of the alternatives likely to be more compatible with the new approach to housing than is our present tax? All things considered, would a basic revision of the American real estate tax be desirable? These are the questions the present study will discuss and attempt to answer.

The effects of taxes on urban housing can be usefully classified as (1) effects on the operation of existing units, (2) effects on the rehabilitation of existing units, and (3) effects on the construction of new units. We wish to limit the analysis, as far as possible, to the first two of these classes of effects, both because they are more closely related than is the third to the new approach to housing and because they have received the least attention elsewhere. We will therefore bring in new construction only to the extent necessary to support the analysis of the other categories. In other words, we will deal with the effect of taxes on that part of urban renewal concerned with the maintenance or improvement of existing housing rather than that part involving new construction.

The plan of the work is as follows: Chapter 2 will define terms and develop a theory of the house-operating firm. Chapter 3 will consider some special problems that arise in analyzing the supply of and demand for housing services. Chapter 4 will deal with the concept of a rental-housing industry made up of the house-operating firms described in Chapter 2. Chapter 5 will analyze the concept of the "slum" in terms suggested by our model of the rental housing industry. Chapter 6 will describe the alternative ways of taxing real estate that

[6] William W. Nash, *Residential Rehabilitation: Private Profits and Public Purposes* (New York, McGraw-Hill, 1959).

have been either tried or suggested in the United States or elsewhere. Chapter 7 will develop a theory of the incidence of these alternative taxes on the operation of rental housing, employing the theoretical model developed in Chapters 2, 3, and 4. Chapter 8 will investigate the theoretical incidence of the same taxes on housing rehabilitation. Chapter 9 will discuss the problem of testing the theoretical conclusions of earlier chapters by reference to existing evidence and will explain why no tests can presently be made. Chapter 10 will review in detail the principal arguments (on grounds other than those covered in earlier chapters) that have been advanced for and against the use of the various alternative real estate taxes; we shall end the chapter and the study by weighing all the arguments and stating our conclusions regarding a basic revision of the American real estate tax.

Chapters 2 through 8 are the heart of this study, since they contain all of the analysis of the effects of alternative real estate taxes on maintenance and rehabilitation. The question of alternatives is raised here precisely because public interest in the housing problem suggests the relevance of considering possible real estate tax reforms. Any policy choice among the alternatives, however, must take into account many other criteria besides effects on maintenance and rehabilitation. Chapter 10 is an attempt to review a number of these other criteria. Within the scope of this study, such a review could not be carried out at the same level of detail as was employed in the central chapters. The last chapter, then, is not intended to be exhaustive, but it serves the purpose of putting the conclusions of Chapters 2 through 8 back into the context of tax policy as a whole.

CHAPTER TWO

THE
HOUSE–OPERATING
FIRM

In order to examine the effects of taxes on the maintenance and rehabilitation of rental housing, we shall require both a theory of the house-operating enterprise and of the rental-housing industry. Very little work has been done by economists on either of these subjects and less on the first than the second.[1] In this chapter we shall develop a theory which regards the building structure as a piece of more or less fixed capital (analogous to a "plant") to which the owner applies variable inputs in the form of operating outlays in order to produce varying outputs of housing service.

One reason for the paucity of economic analyses of the rental-housing firm may be the widely acknowledged difficulty of measuring the output of housing services. This problem has

[1] The most useful works consulted on the economic theory of housing were Herbert W. Robinson, *The Economics of Building* (London, P. S. King, 1939); Sherman J. Maisel, *An Approach to the Problems of Analysing Housing Demand,* Doctoral Dissertation, Harvard University, 1948 (unpublished); Chester Rapkin, Louis Winnick, and David M. Blank, *Housing Market Analysis* (Washington, D.C., Housing and Home Finance Agency, 1953); and Wallace F. Smith, *An Outline Theory of the Housing Market, with Special Reference to Low-Income Housing and Urban Renewal,* Doctoral Dissertation, University of Washington, 1958 (unpublished). Ralph Turvey, *The Economics of Real Property: An Analysis of Property Values and Patterns of Use* (New York, Macmillan, 1957), proved useful on many aspects of real estate economics but does not deal with the house-operating industry per se. William G. Grigsby's important book, *Housing Markets and Public Policy* (Philadelphia, University of Pennsylvania Press, 1963), appeared after this study was substantially completed.

long confounded analysts of housing. None of the available (nor even the conceivable) data on housing characteristics accurately measure the output of housing services. Quantitative measures such as number of rental units, number of rooms, or square footage or floor space overlook the obvious qualitative differences between one unit and another. Direct qualitative measures are nonexistent; indirect ones such as existence or extent of plumbing, heating, electric lighting, and so on are used in the decennial Census of Housing as a rough measure of the quality of housing space. But these indicators obviously do not cut fine enough to establish more than a few quality classes. Moreover, we are left wondering, first, how to weigh and combine the various indicated quality characteristics and, second, how to combine any overall quality index with a quantity factor to measure total housing service. In short, physical quality indicators do not make possible an ordinal, much less a cardinal, ranking of housing service outputs.[2]

Occupancy introduces additional difficulties. Ernest M. and Robert M. Fisher point out that "real estate market behaviour centers about a fixed capacity to produce services (the standing stock) and a variable intensity of using it through time." [3] Therefore, if the analyst takes the available number of units in the standing stock of housing or in a given structure as the basis for the quantity factor in output of services, he overlooks the problem of vacancy and of intensity of use. Vacancy is a simple enough concept: if a unit is not occupied, it is vacant and is therefore rendering no services. Intensity of use, as developed by Fisher and Fisher, is a more complex notion, with a quality as well as a quantity aspect: if two people occupy an apartment, is it yielding twice as much service as if one person occupies it, or does the higher density reduce the "quality" of service to

---

[2] A Census of Housing has been incorporated in each Decennial Census of the United States, starting in 1940. In addition to tabulating the existence or extent of various kinds of equipment that may be taken to reflect "quality," the 1940 Census classified units as either "needing major repairs" or not, the 1950 Census as either "dilapidated" or not, and the 1960 Census as "sound," "deteriorating," or "dilapidated," in an effort to record overall condition.

[3] *Urban Real Estate* (New York, Holt, 1954), p. 184.

each so that the total output with two occupants is less than twice as much as with one? In the analysis that follows, it will be seen that our way of handling output automatically takes vacancies into account, so that we need not specify the vacancy rates in the course of our argument. On the other hand, we make no allowance for intensity of use in the sense of density of occupancy, on the ground that the concept is not relevant here. We assume the existence of occupancy codes that establish the maximum permissible density per room, but we take no account of the possible variations in density that can occur within the legal limits.

Fisher and Fisher conclude, "No one has yet developed a satisfactory unit of measure of inventory capacity, intensity of use, or rate of utilization." [4] In this and the ensuing chapters we shall attempt to get around the problem by arguing that two observable quantities—gross rent receipts or total annual cost of a property—can be used under appropriate conditions to give us an ordinal ranking of all that property's possible outputs of housing service. We hope to show that this ordinal ranking allows us to answer the question we have posed: what are the effects of alternative systems of real estate taxation on the maintenance and rehabilitation of urban rental housing?

In analyzing the house-operating firm, we shall make use of several simplifying assumptions:

1. All properties are owned debt-free, so that we need not distinguish between the owner's equity in a property and its value.

2. The marginal cost to the owner of accommodating an added tenant is zero.[5]

3. All apartment units in each structure are identical, so

---

4 *Ibid.*, p. 185.

5 While the total cost of operating a building might be reduced significantly if occupancy fell from 100 percent to, say, 60 percent, it seems reasonable to assume that it is not affected by variations within the normal range of 90 to 100 percent actually encountered in most markets. Much the same point is made by Rapkin, Winnick, and Blank in setting up their model for the analysis of the housing market (*Housing Market Analysis*, p. 22).

that we may speak of "rent per unit" as a single figure representing the rent of each apartment in a given building.

4. There is no business or building cycle to contend with.

Concepts and symbols will be defined as they are introduced. Subscripts L or B with any symbol will indicate that part attributable, respectively, to land or building.

The objective of the owner of rental housing is to maximize his net income from the property, not in any one year but over the whole life of the investment. The property itself consists of land and a building. The land we regard as immutable. The building can be regarded as very durable but not immutable physical capital. In the course of time it is subject to wear and tear, which can be repaired by suitable reinvestment. It can also be changed into a different piece of physical capital by investment in remodeling. For any given state of the building as a physical structure there is a set of different ways of operating it which will affect the rents the owner can obtain.

The operator of a rental housing firm thus makes two kinds of decisions:

1. *Operating decisions.* These regulate the amount of variable inputs to be applied to the physical structure. The variable inputs include such expenses as cleaning costs; outlays or allowances for painting and decorating; cost of providing heat; cost of minor repairs; outlays for janitors, handymen, porters, elevator operators, and doormen, if any; and, to some extent, costs of administration. These are expenses we include under the heading "operating costs," symbolized by OC. Each is to some degree variable in the short run, and, provided the outlays are combined rationally, the higher the combined total, the higher the level of quality of operation of the building. Thus, in the short run the owner varies his output of housing services by varying its quality, and, as we shall argue, up to a point the higher the quality, the higher his rent receipts will be.

Setting the level of rent to be charged per unit is also a short-run decision.

2. *Investment decisions.* The owner always has before him the possibility of altering the physical layout of his building

by remodeling it. Since the expense of remodeling is considerable, the cost can only be recouped over a number of years, and the expense must be thought of as an investment. At this point it is important to define "remodeling" carefully. At any moment a rental building contains a given number of apartments of given layout and contains a given inventory of physical equipment such as elevators, wiring, and plumbing. Remodeling takes place whenever the owner either changes the layout of interior space or adds equipment to that already installed. By this definition the replacement of an old bathtub by a new one is not remodeling, but the installation of an additional bathtub is.

Choosing the rate at which to replace worn-out physical equipment will also be treated as an investment decision, inasmuch as it also involves a very long planning horizon. The exact point, however, at which one draws the line between maintenance, which is a current expense, and replacement, which is a capital expenditure, is merely a convention.

Both kinds of investment decisions affect the physical structure of the building. They may be thought of as long-run decisions, since they involve a long planning period, or time horizon.

Both investment and operating decisions are subject to constraints imposed by various local legal codes: the owner is required by building, sanitary, and fire codes to meet certain minimum standards both as to elements of structure and provision of operating services. But he retains one degree of freedom: if he does not wish to comply or to sell to another owner who will do so, he can simply board up, raze, or abandon his building.

In the United States the owner of a building usually owns the land beneath it as well. The analysis of the incidence of real estate taxes, however, requires that we be able to separate the rent or value of land from that of improvements. (The problems this separation raises are treated in later chapters.) From the owner's point of view, such a separation is irrelevant in the short run. It becomes necessary only in connection with the long-run decision whether or not to raze the building.[6]

Our object in this study is to examine the effects of alternative real estate taxes on the existing stock of rental housing. As the analysis above suggests, the problem is best divided into two parts: the effects of taxes, first, on short-run operating decisions and, second, on long-run investment decisions. But before we can take up the effects of taxes (in Chapters 6 through 9), we must develop the model of firm and industry in some detail. We shall examine short-run operating decisions first.

In order to develop an economic model of the building as an operating unit, let us suppose that we have an experimentally inclined property owner in possession of a single apartment house. This owner wishes to earn the largest possible return from his house. Let us here assume that the owner's decisions as to the physical structure of the house have already been made. He is satisfied that no conceivable remodeling would pay. With the physical structure as it stands, he wishes to find the most profitable way to operate.

What the owner must do, then, is vary his operating outlay and rent per unit from time to time and observe the results on his income statement. (To isolate these results, we assume that outlays and rents charged by all other building operators remain fixed.) Higher levels of outlay by our single operator produce higher qualities of housing service. The maximum quantity of service that the building can produce is fixed by its structure, that is, by the number of rental units it contains. Since the maximum quantity is fixed, the maximum total output of service varies directly with quality. The actual output will fall short of the maximum by the percentage of vacancies, if any.

How much scope does the owner have for varying operating outlays in a given building? It is obvious to anyone who reflects for a moment on the nature of the services provided by housing that a house is an extraordinarily complex entity. Accounting concepts such as operating and maintenance expense

[6] See Turvey, *Economics of Real Property*, pp. 22–24.

and economic concepts such as output therefore take on subtle-
ties and ambiguities when applied to housing that are not
present when one discusses ordinary machinery. The quality
of a building, considered as a place in which to live, depends
upon many elements of maintenance and operation that are
within the landlord's legal power to vary. The number of men
employed in the building is one such variable factor—a building with a full-time superintendent or a doorman is considered
to be of higher quality than a similar one without. The amount
of heat provided, above the legal minimum, is another variable
that affects the quality of the building as a residence. Does a
porter collect the garbage from each apartment once a day?
Twice a day? Or do the tenants have to carry it to the basement
themselves? Are the public halls mopped weekly, monthly, or
only when the Building Department inspector has announecd
his impending visit? Again, services affecting the quality of
residence in a building can be varied widely by the landlord
within limits imposed by the housing or sanitary codes.

Even administrative costs are not immutable. A landlord who
is operating on a shoestring may own half a dozen tenements
which he administers personally and without benefit of an
office. His tenants will find it very difficult and time-consuming
to locate him. (Sometimes even the courts cannot find him.)
When tenants do find him, he may be too busy to attend to
their complaints at once. On the other hand, a landlord operating quality apartment houses will need an office and sizable
administrative staff to give his tenants the prompt service they
expect. Again the expense is variable, and the quality of service
offered varies directly with it.

Just as higher levels of quality cost the owner more to produce, so they will command higher rents. The owner will find
operation most profitable at the point at which gross rents
exceed operating costs by the largest absolute margin. Any
rational owner will try to operate a rental property at such a
maximum profit point, which we call the "optimum level of
quality of operation." Although the owner cannot observe or
directly measure his building's output of housing service, he

can readily observe and measure his gross rents and his costs. From these, provided he can establish some regular relationship between them, he can find the most profitable operating point.

Note also that a real estate owner can readily see the way in which his competitors operate their buildings. It requires only casual observation for him to discover what they consider to be the most profitable level of operating outlay on properties similar to his.

We must now try to establish a reasonable hypothesis as to the relationship between gross rent receipts and total cost for any single rental housing structure. Let us construct a diagram (Figure 2.1) in which we plot gross rents and costs on the

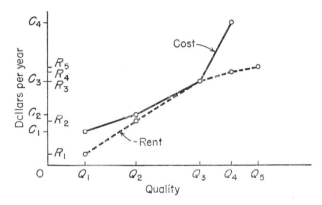

FIGURE 2.1   GROSS RENT, TOTAL COST, AND QUALITY
IN A SINGLE STRUCTURE

vertical axis. We attach ordinal but not cardinal significance to the positions of points along the horizontal scale; quality increases as we move from left to right, but the amount or proportion by which it increases is left unspecified.

The gross rents (R), measured in dollars per year on the vertical scale, require little discussion. They are simply the annual rents which the owner receives when he operates the building at any given level of quality long enough so that each lease brings in the going market rental for space of that quality.

The appropriate concept of costs for the diagram is more

difficult to describe. Costs (C) are put on an average annual basis and are the sum of annual operating cost (OC) and what, for want of a better term, we shall call annual fixed cost (FC). The latter, in turn, consists of planned net income (N) plus an annual charge for replacement (D). For the present we assume that there are no taxes on the property or on the income it yields.

Planned net income (N) is included as a cost merely on conventional grounds. It equals the net annual income before taxes expected by an investor when he buys or builds a property. Perhaps it is unusual to employ the concept of net income *before* taxes. We do so in order to facilitate the later graphic analysis of the effects of introducing alternative real estate taxes into the system.

In a competitive market for real estate as an investment, bids for income-producing properties will tend to bring their market prices to a level at which properties in a similar category (e.g., apartment buildings involving similar risks) will sell to yield a similar rate of return. Thus, planned net income and what may be called a normal profit tend toward equality. Since planned net income is defined as a cost, the owner is earning a normal profit when $R = C$.

The definition of D, a charge for replacement, differs from the usual accounting concept of depreciation. Included in D are the average annual outlays for replacement of structure and parts needed to keep a building in a given average state of repair or condition.[7] We regard the choice of an appropriate level of replacement expenditure as a long-run investment decision. Hence, further discussion of D is postponed until the last section of this chapter, which deals with such decisions.

In the short run, D (and hence the "condition of structure") being regarded as fixed, the owner's objective is to maximize

---

[7] Real estate analysts commonly draw a distinction between the accounting concept of depreciation, as developed under the influence of income-tax regulations, and a class of actual outlays for replacement in some respects similar to D as defined here. See, for example, Richard U. Ratcliff, *Real Estate Analysis* (New York, McGraw-Hill, 1961), pp. 109–10.

the spread between rent and operating costs. How will our "experimentally inclined property owner" go about it? The answer is that the first dollar he spends on operation of the building he will use to buy that operating input which adds the largest increment of quality to the service he is selling. As he moves from lower to higher levels of cost, he moves progressively from more to less "quality-productive" dollars. The quality produced by each dollar he cannot observe, but he assumes that it is measured by the observable increase in rents which it permits him to obtain. Thus, each point on the cost curve in Figure 2.1 represents the least cost of producing the corresponding quality of output, i.e., the corresponding amount of rent. And we are here assuming that each owner can define such a curve for his building, that, in other words, he is aware of the most productive order in which to add his variable inputs. If this be granted, then we have a curve which defines the associated changes in cost and quality whether the landlord is moving up to higher costs or down to lower.

It may be objected that some of the amenities which the owner can provide are interdependent and that as a result he will not be able to proceed continuously from more to less quality-productive dollars. For example, suppose that for technical reasons amenity B cannot be introduced until after amenity A has been provided but that B produces $1.50 of rent per dollar of cost, while A produces only $1.25. Our economic logic then requires the owner to install B before A, but technical considerations forbid this. Does this demolish our hypothetical systematic rent-cost-quality relationship? The answer is that it does not. The owner will in such a case obviously treat A and B as a single amenity, for if ever it paid to introduce A, it would pay to introduce B simultaneously. Insisting that such interdependent elements of quality be treated as a single element in no way diminishes the predictive power of the analysis.

We believe that it is not unreasonable to assume that for each building there is a known best order for changes in service. The facts are consistent with this assumption in that one ob-

serves among apartment buildings in a large city a similarity
of services offered by buildings of approximately the same type
and location: one does not find doormen or well-furnished
lobbies in buildings that are otherwise slums, nor does one
observe any absence of doormen or of elegant lobbies in the
larger apartment houses on New York's Fifth Avenue. There
is a clearly marked order in which services are added or sub-
tracted by owners wishing to raise or lower the quality of
their buildings.

A second complex problem is the time dimension of the
cost-quality curve. If an owner decides to reduce his variable
outlays on a building, a decline in quality may follow at once
in a single leap or it may occur only gradually with the passage
of time, depending upon what outlays he eliminates. For example, if he fires the doorman, the building drops immediately
to a lower quality level. On the other hand, if he decides to
cut costs by repainting the lobby and halls every ten years
instead of every five years, the time required to move to a new
quality level is obviously longer.

What the cost-quality curve shows is the level of quality that
can be continuously maintained if the owner continues to make
the indicated cost outlays over a period at least as long as the
useful life of the longest-lived element purchased by his variable outlays. Hence, movements from one point to another on
the curve must be thought of as sometimes taking a number of
years to complete. Nor does the curve necessarily describe the
path between any two points during a period of transition.

If movements from point to point on the cost-quality curve
take anywhere from a day to, say, ten years, are we dealing
with a long-run curve? The answer is "No." In economics the
long run is usually defined as a period just long enough for
all productive factors to become variable. In the case of industrial plant and equipment, life expectancy—and hence the
long run—is on the order of twenty or thirty years. But capital
invested in housing has an indefinitely long life expectancy;
the long run is here very long indeed. It is, in fact, the longev-
ity of physical structures, together with their immobility and

their adaptability, that gives urban real estate economics its unique character. Thus, in the context of the urban economy, the cost-quality curve expresses what is logically a short-run relationship.

Figure 2.1 is a diagram of gross rent, total cost, and quality in a single structure. Rent and cost are given in dollars per year. We have plotted four total-cost points; the levels of cost for these are marked off on the vertical scale as C_1 through C_4.

C_1 represents the level of annual fixed costs: at C_1 the owner spends nothing on operating the building. Needless to say, this is an unlikely state of affairs: although the building has equipment—perhaps a furnace and an elevator—none of the equipment operates because the owner is unwilling to spend anything for electricity, oil, or superintendence. The quality of service produced at C_1 we denote as Q_1. Q_1 is not an attractive prospect to tenants; they are willing to pay for it no more than R_1 in gross rent. The property operates at a loss, since R_1 is less than annual fixed costs, C_1.

At C_1 our owner is probably violating most of the local housing and sanitary codes. To conform with all the codes, he must add to his costs an average annual amount sufficient to bring the total to C_2. This produces services of quality Q_2, and, as we have drawn the diagram, tenants are now willing to pay gross rents of R_2, which greatly reduce the owner's loss.

If the owner raises his variable maintenance and other operating outlays further, bringing total cost up to C_3, he discovers that he has increased the quality of the building's output sufficiently to command gross rents of R_3; rent and cost are now equal, and since planned net income, equal to a normal rate of return, is included as a cost, the owner is now earning a normal return on his investment.

Beyond Q_3, however, the relationship between cost and rent reverses: costs now increase faster than rent. If the owner attempts to raise quality further, he can do so, but his net return will diminish and finally disappear because tenants are not willing to pay much more than R_4 to live in this particular building, no matter how elaborately it is operated. This is not an arbitrary assumption of our theory but a logical result of the distinction between structure, design, and layout on the one hand and operating outlays on the other. (Moreover, the point is supported by the testimony of professional property managers.[8]) The original structure imposes limitations. No one will pay high rents to live in an old tenement simply because the owner cleans it up and supplies a doorman. If the owner wishes to remodel an old building, that is a different story, but in our terms it is also a different structure.

We are therefore justified in assuming that there is some maximum quality of service that can be wrung from our given structure by spending infinite sums on its operation. This limit we mark off as Q_5. This quality would be approached asymptotically as cost outlays approached infinity, but the maximum rent that our structure can bring in at Q_5 is decidedly finite and can be designated R_5. In short, we have an economic application of the rule, "You can't make a silk purse out of a sow's ear."

If the cost and revenue curves for a given structure are related in the way we have described, it follows that a rational building owner will try to operate at the optimum level of quality of operation, the level at which the excess of gross rent over total cost is maximized or of total cost over gross rent minimized. Such a point will satisfy the condition that an additional dollar spent annually on operation will enable the owner to procure just one additional dollar of gross rent.

In Figure 2.1 we used an ordinal scale of quality as a crutch for the exposition. In fact, the crutch is unnecessary and may be misleading. It would be misleading, for example, if it led one to suppose that any significance could be attached to the slope of either curve in the diagram, for the ordinal scale can obviously be stretched or compressed between any two points

8 James C. Downs writes, "In other words, there is a point of diminishing return in the installation of added values—a point at which better equipment or accomodation fails to be economic—a point at which even the installation of gold door knobs would not bring a higher price." *Principles of Real Estate Management* (Chicago, Institute of Real Estate Management, 1950), p. 72. See additional quotations from property managers in Chapter 9 of this book.

without altering the ordinal ranking. Yet each such manipulation changes the apparent slope of the curves. In fact, the curves in Figure 2.1 have no slope in the ordinary sense of that word.

The information contained in Figure 2.1 consists of three elements: (1) an hypothesis concerning the relationship between quality and total cost, (2) an hypothesis concerning the relationship between quality and gross rent, and (3) by derivation from (1) and (2) a relationship between gross rent and total cost.

The same information can be presented in a diagram showing the relationship between gross rent and total cost directly, as in Figure 2.2. The presentation employed in Figure 2.2 has

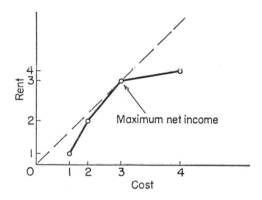

FIGURE 2.2   THE REVENUE-COST CURVE

the logical advantage of showing only the data that are observable to the building operator. He does not observe quality but only cost and rent. But because quality increases with cost and rent increases with quality, he is behaving *as if* he could observe ordinal differences in quality; that is to say, his behavior is exactly the same as it would be if he *could* observe such differences.

In Figure 2.2 we measure annual gross rent along the vertical scale and average annual cost outlays along the horizontal. We plot the same points as in Figure 2.1, but this time we associate each cost level directly with the rent it makes attainable. For simplicity the resulting function will be called a revenue-cost curve. By drawing a 45-degree diagonal through the origin, we can distinguish the points at which gross rent equals annual cost from those at which it does not. Since normal profits are included in annual cost, the diagonal obviously represents points of normal profit. Net income above normal is measured by either the vertical or the horizontal distance from a point above the diagonal to the diagonal. A net loss (as a deduction from the normal profit) is measured by either of those distances from a point below the diagonal to the diagonal.

In Figure 2.3 we have generalized the revenue-cost rela-

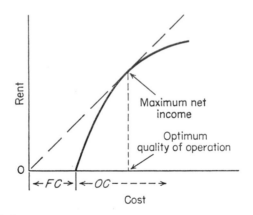

FIGURE 2.3   THE REVENUE-COST CURVE—CONTINUOUS CASE

tionship into a smooth curve. For the sake of simplicity we have also introduced the not implausible assumption that rent falls to zero when operating cost falls to zero. This means that the point of intersection of the revenue-cost curve and the horizontal axis conveniently divides fixed cost (to the left) from operating cost (to the right).

A major difference between the curves in Figure 2.1 and the revenue-cost curves of Figures 2.2 and 2.3 is that we can attach meaning to the slope of the latter two. This slope, dR/dC, is the ratio of a small change in revenue to the change in cost necessary to bring it about. The building operator will earn his maximum profit at the point where this ratio, and hence the slope, is unity. At such a point, the revenue-cost curve is parallel to the diagonal and, when normal profits are earned, will be tangent to it.

The above rule for locating the owner's optimum point is valid as long as we draw revenue-cost curves with constantly diminishing slope. Increasing slope would mean, of course, increasing returns of revenue to increments of cost, not that revenue is rising more than cost in absolute amount—which is shown by any slope greater than 45 degrees—but that the ratio between the increments is rising. We have not shown such a region, because our definition of the cost function rules it out. According to that definition, the owner, if he is increasing his cost outlays, proceeds in order from the most to the least productive variable expenses. If he wishes to decrease costs, he reverses the order. Hence, the revenue-cost curve, as we define it, cannot have increasing slope. Shifts in relative costs of inputs or changes in technology or taste might alter the ratio of added rent to added cost for various services, but this would not create regions of increasing returns. Instead it would lead owners to rearrange the order in which services would be taken up, creating a new revenue-cost curve that would preserve decreasing returns. Each revenue-cost curve is specific to a particular structure maintained in a particular condition and to a particular state of taste, technology, prices, incomes, and household numbers.

Thus far we have simplified the argument by ignoring the fact that gross rent can be further analyzed into three components of which it is the product: rent per unit (p), rate of occupancy (r), and number of units in the structure (U). For any given structure, these three variables can be reduced to two: since the number of units in the building is constant, it can be multiplied by the rate of occupancy to give the number of occupied units (U_0). Moreover, $U_0 = R/p$. Therefore, we can employ a three-dimensional diagram for any given structure to show R, p, and C and derive from it the implicit values of U_0.

We have drawn such a diagram in Figure 2.4. Essentially,

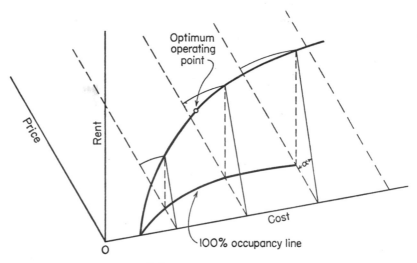

FIGURE 2.4   PRICE, RENT, AND COST

this is the R/C curve of Figure 2.3, with a third dimension added for price. The result is a diagram showing gross rent in a given building as a function of rent per unit, p, and cost, C, taken to represent quality.[9] The height of the surface thus generated above the horizontal plane through the origin is the total gross rent, R. At any point on the surface the height, R, divided by the price, p, is the tangent of an angle a (see Fig. 2-4), and this tangent is therefore the value of U_0 for the given point. The optimum operating point (maximum profit) is that point on the surface at which R most exceeds (or falls least short of) C. At such a point the surface will have a slope in the cost direction of unity $(dR/dC=1)$.

The shape of the surface can be explained as follows: For any given cost, and hence quality, as price increases, a point

---

[9] As explained in note 5 of this chapter, it is assumed that cost does not vary with occupancy.

is reached beyond which occupancy falls below 100 percent. Up to that point, as price increases, R increases proportionately, since occupancy remains at 100 percent. Therefore, the front side of the surface, as it is drawn, is a plane rising from the horizontal plane through the origin at angle a, and $\tan a = U_0$. Up to the point where occupancy falls below 100 percent, the ratio between changes in R and changes in p is U_0, the constant number of occupied units in the building.

If we continue to increase p beyond the point of 100 percent occupancy, what happens to R? If the elasticity of demand for space in the building were less than unity, R would continue to rise as p rose. If the elasticity were greater than unity, R would fall as p rose beyond the 100 percent occupancy point. Much depends then on the degree of elasticity of demand for space in single buildings. Since we have no direct evidence on this point, we have made use of indirect evidence, leading to a conclusion that elasticity is greater than unity (although not infinite, since buildings are differentiated) and that gross rent is maximized at the highest price which will just keep the building fully rented.

Evidence on this point is of two sorts: first, the testimony of property managers, such as Downs, who assert that the rental schedule is best set to obtain close to 100 percent occupancy,[10] and second, the evidence presented by Rapkin, Winnick, and Blank that whenever marketwide occupancy falls below a critical level of about 95 percent, owners of large rental structures begin to cut rents.[11] If demand for space in individual structures were inelastic at prices above that which gives 100 percent occupancy, it would be normal to find occupancy rates well below 100 percent in equilibrium situations, for landlords would there be earning maximum gross rents. Instead, one finds rents falling soon after occupancy drops be-

10 *Real Estate Management*, pp. 69–70.

11 *Housing Market Analysis*, pp. 22–28. The idea of a critical level is presented but less thoroughly examined in earlier works on housing by Ernest M. Fisher, *Urban Real Estate Markets: Characteristics and Financing* (New York, National Bureau of Economic Research, 1951), p. 98, and Downs, *Real Estate Management*, pp. 20–25.

low, say, 95 percent; and occupancy rates below 90 percent in any area are considered a mark of dangerous oversupply. The fact that the critical level is around 95 percent instead of 99.9 percent (in the Rapkin, Winnick, and Blank analysis) or that landlords do not avoid *all* vacancies by following an appropriate rent policy (in the Downs analysis) does not contradict our inference concerning elasticity. In the former case, the lag can be explained by the fact that it is difficult to lower rents to attract new tenants while keeping them high for old tenants, yet it is undesirable to lower rents for all tenants when there are only a few vacancies and the owner is uncertain how difficult they will be to fill, because if rents are lowered too much, they cannot at once be raised again. In the latter case, one must bear in mind the combination of normal turnover plus normal time lag in renting vacant units. These two factors alone suffice to explain a considerable number of vacancies at any one moment. (Even if he gave away space rent-free, a landlord would have some turnover—since tenants are neither permanently rooted in one town nor immortal.)

Occupancy rates below 95 percent have frequently been observed and have often persisted for years, but we take this to be a result of the building cycle or of the general business cycle, and our analysis attempts to abstract from these conditions. Suffice it to say that when, for example, real income falls drastically, vacancies may persist despite the fact that owners reduce rent per unit, because rents will never be reduced below the floor set by operating costs. Even to reduce them that far would require many years of downward cyclical pressure, but analysis of such cyclical movements is outside the scope of this book.

Finally, the nature of the rental-housing market in large cities where there are numerous buildings competing for tenants is consistent with the notion that demand for space in any one building will be price-elastic. And if this conclusion is granted, then the maximum gross rent obtainable at any one quality of operation is at that price per unit which is just low enough to give 100 percent occupancy. Or, to put it the other way around, the locus of highest price 100 percent occupancy points is also the locus of maximum gross-rent points.

Continuing to examine the gross-rent surface, consider how it behaves for any given price as cost and quality of operation increase. We find that for any given price, occupancy and gross rent increase as cost and quality rise—for more tenants can be attracted as quality improves. But once we reach 100 percent occupancy, gross rent, of course, cannot increase further despite further increases in quality—the price plane intersects the surface in a horizontal line.

The maximum price at which occupancy is 100 percent increases as cost increases but at a decreasing rate, for one approaches a limit beyond which it is impossible to obtain higher rent from a given structure by adding amenities. As the surface stretches out to the northeast, its height above the zero rent plane gradually levels off and approaches the horizontal.

It is now evident that our two-dimensional R/C curve of Figure 2.3 was simply the projection on the R/C plane of the ridge line of the gross rent surface. Since occupancy is 100 percent at all points along this ridge line, nothing of importance is lost if we use the two- rather than the three-dimensional diagram. The best obtainable prices can be read off the diagram in place of gross rent by dividing the values of R by the number of units in the building.

Having examined the owner's short-run operating decisions, we shall now turn to his long-run investment decisions. These concern four matters: (1) the price to be paid for a property when buying it as an investment; (2) the rate at which to replace worn out elements of structure and equipment, i.e., replacement policy; (3) whether and how to remodel the building; and (4) whether or not to raze it (a subject we do not, however, deal with in this chapter). We omit consideration of the possibility that the owner will sell the building to another operator, since in that case we simply have a different operator whose decisions on the other matters are relevant.

Concerning the first investment decision, the price to be

paid for a property, we start with the point that an investor buying a rental property consisting of land and a building will pay for it, at most, an amount equal to the present value of the expected future net income.[12] If real estate were not subject to special taxation, the relevant net income figure would be N as we have defined it—that is to say, planned net income remaining after the necessary annual allowance for replacement, D, has been deducted but before any conventional charge for depreciation. When real estate is taxed, the expected tax charges are deducted from planned net income, and the maximum purchase price is the present value of the expected remainder. The rate of discount used in calculating present value is the rate of return obtainable on alternative properties of the type in question. Realized net income is, of course, a residual and may be either more or less than planned net income at the time of purchase.

What can we say about the time pattern of expected future returns? In connection with capital invested in ordinary machinery, it is often plausible to assume that the machine will yield a net return of N in each year of its life and that after L years it falls apart all at once (the "one-hoss shay" assumption). But this attractive simplification is not satisfactory for real property, for buildings have a very long, in a sense an indefinite, life expectancy. Some last only thirty or forty years, some go on for thousands. It would be contrary to observed fact to assume that they go on producing exactly the same services and income year by year from beginning to end.

The problem is further complicated for two reasons: first, in reality each separate part of a structure has a life expectancy of its own; second, there is no logical dividing line (but only a conventional one) between repairs, which are classified as an operating outlay, and replacement of worn-out structure and equipment, which is classified as an investment. It might seem simple enough to declare that repairs to parts are operating expenses, while replacement of a part is a capital outlay. But

12 Turvey, *Economics of Real Property*, pp. 8–9.

this language begs the question, which turns upon the definition of a "part." For example, putting a new pane of glass in a window would be considered an operating repair if the whole window were defined as a part but would be a capital outlay if the pane of glass itself were defined as a part. This illustration also shows that the useful life of an item cannot help to clarify the distinction, for panes of glass often have a useful life longer than the window in which they are set.

Nor does the size of the outlay provide a distinction. Pointing up an outside wall is a fairly expensive job which is, nevertheless, generally considered a repair. A new bathroom sink, though it costs much less, is generally classified as a capital item. But an arbitrary line must be drawn somewhere, so for the present we will simply assume that a clear distinction can be made between repairs and replacements, the former to be considered operating expenses, the latter investments of capital.

The owner of an existing building has to make investment decisions because with the passage of time his building may suffer not only physical deterioration but also various other kinds of capital erosion. As a rational profit-seeker, he must decide whether, when, and how to meet this erosion. We can distinguish four principal ways in which the capital value of a building may be worn away:

1. Equipment and some parts of the structure wear out, even though they have been regularly repaired. We will call this "physical erosion."

2. Most buildings are eventually overtaken by what has been called "design obsolescence." This is a complex phenomenon resulting from improvements in building technology, from changes in architectural style, from the development of new home appliances which older buildings do not readily accommodate, and from changes in the economics of housekeeping.

3. Buildings may suffer capital erosion if they become superfluous in the bracket of the rental market for which they were designed. This can occur for a number of reasons, among

which are a change in the number, size distribution, or income distribution of families or a change in the proportion of families wishing to own rather than rent their homes. We will call this "market obsolescence."

4. A building may suffer capital erosion if the neighborhood in which it stands changes so that the building no longer has the optimum set of characteristics for the market in that neighborhood. We will call this "neighborhood obsolescence."

Although these four kinds of erosion often occur simultaneously, they are analytically distinct. In many cases their effects can be offset, however, either wholly or in part, by appropriate investment decisions. Consider physical erosion first. How can we encompass this complex process in a simplified model? Two obvious possibilities suggest themselves. On the one hand, we might assume that none of the structure is replaced as it wears out, so that the building gradually deteriorates and is finally razed. On the other hand, we might assume that the owner reinvests enough capital in the building so that each part is replaced as it wears out and the building has perpetual life.

These are, however, merely two among a wide range of other possibilities which can be summed up in the most general way by saying that the owner of a building can choose not only the level of quality at which he wishes to operate a building but more broadly the level at which he wishes to maintain its structure. For example, he can, if he thinks it will be profitable, let a building deteriorate from high quality (at high rents) to mediocre quality (at moderate rents) and then arrest further deterioration—leveling off, so to speak, at the mediocre state. (How this can be done will emerge below.) Or, conversely, he can buy a mediocre building and restore it to a level of high quality at which it will command high rents. In this connection one thinks of remodeling, certainly a common enough practice. But in principle there is no reason why an owner could not simply renew worn-out elements to restore the original structure exactly as it was. The most general case, then, recognizes that a rental structure can be moved, within certain limits, from one rent class into another, either up or down, depending upon possibilities for profit indicated by the market.[13]

Among the constraints limiting this movement is the fact that the building is physically rooted and hence cannot escape the influence of its neighborhood considered as environment nor the advantages and disadvantages of its location with respect to other neighborhoods. A second set of constraints is imposed by housing, sanitary, and fire codes, which are intended to prevent a building from deteriorating physically below certain prescribed standards.

Within these limits, how, precisely, can the owner vary the level at which he maintains a structure? The answer is that he does so by varying the period (L) after which he replaces the physical parts that are subject to erosion. The process is analogous to that of trading in an automobile. If you trade it every year, you are always driving a new car. You will get better transportation service that way than if you trade the car in every five years, but it will cost you more as well.

The "one-hoss shay" assumption is just as clearly inapplicable to real property and its equipment as it is to an automobile. The plumbing in an apartment house, for example, deteriorates gradually with time. After, say, twenty-five years the pipes still work, but the water pressure is likely to be much reduced. Yet it may be possible to avoid replacing them for fifty years if the owner wishes to conduct his business that way. Much the same thing can be said of many of the physical elements in a building that wear out with time. Thus, the building owner can vary the condition of a given structure within limits imposed by its layout and equipment by varying the average L which he attributes to its parts.

The term $1/L$ may be called the "rate of replacement" of

13 The idea that buildings can be moved from one rental class to another was apparently first recognized as a necessary element in a systematic market theory by Herbert W. Robinson. He put it thus: "The number of buildings in any one class can be altered, not only by new building, but by transformation of buildings by repairs and alterations in other rental classes." *Economics of Building,* p. 83.

The same concept is employed by Maisel, *Analysing Housing Demand,* Chap. IV, who acknowledges Robinson's prior development of the idea.

structure. Of course, if an owner elects to move a building by changing this rate, he will probably find it profitable to change the services provided by operating outlays at the same time, since for each given state of the building as structure there is given a different R/C curve. For any given level of operating outlay, one would expect rents to be lower, the lower the rate of replacement of structure.

The actual replacement outlays, D, needed to maintain a structure in a given average condition obviously depend not only on the rate at which structure is replaced but also on the cost of the structural elements themselves. The relevant cost here is not the original construction cost of the building when new, for, among other things, the building may subsequently have been remodeled, which cuts the link to original construction cost even if the relative prices of all structural elements are assumed constant over time. Neither does the price paid for an old building, assuming one could separate it from the price of the land, measure the cost of the structural elements subject to replacement, since a building that cost $1 million to build may soon be selling for $750,000 because of design, neighborhood, or market obsolescence, none of which reduces the cost of the structure that must be kept in being. Nor is the cost of constructing the building anew, as it stands after any remodeling, a true measure of the cost of the structural elements to be replaced. First of all, some elements may never require replacement. Secondly, piece-by-piece replacement of parts over a period of many years cannot be expected to cost the same amount as the same work done all at once. There is thus no way of linking directly to previously described costs the sum which is to be multiplied by $1/L$ to arrive at the annual charge for replacement, D. We can only say that this cost is related to but not equal to the cost of reconstructing the building with its present design, layout, and equipment.

What are the criteria for choosing the optimum rate of replacement of structure? Assume to begin with that no taxes are levied on real estate. The more rapidly structure is replaced, the better its condition and the higher the rent tenants will pay, other things remaining the same. At the same time, the higher the rate of replacement of structure, the higher the annual cost of replacement, D. For example, using straight-line depreciation, if a given piece of equipment with an original cost of $100 is to be replaced over a period of ten years, the annual charge is $10.00, if over six years, $16.67, if over five years, $20.00. (See Table 2.1.) Given that more rapid re-

TABLE 2.1

*Hypothetical Results of Varying Rate of
Replacement of Structure* [a]

Rate of Replacement (1/L)	Annual Replacement Cost (D)	Marginal Cost of Increasing Rate of Replacement	Marginal Increase in Annual Rent Obtained by Increasing Rate of Replacement
1/8	$ 12.5	...	$ 7
1/7	14.3	$ 1.8	6
1/6	16.7	2.4	5
1/5	20.0	3.3	4
1/4	25.0	5.0	3
1/3	33.3	8.3	2
1/2	50.0	16.7	1
1/1	100.0	50.0	0

[a] Assume a structural element with a replacement cost of $100. If L is the assumed life of the element, then the annual charge for replacement (D) is given by $100 \times 1/L$.

placement will enable the owner to command higher rents but will also entail higher costs, the most profitable rate of replacement is that at which the last additional dollar spent annually for more rapid replacement enables the owner to earn just one additional dollar of annual rent. Using the above cost figures, if replacing the given piece of equipment every five years instead of every six enables the owner to command $4.00 of additional rent per year, then it will just pay him to do so, since the additional $4.00 of rent will be bought at a cost of $3.33 of additional annual replacement outlay.

Thus, the owner finds his optimum rate of replacement at that point at which a curve representing the marginal cost of increasing the rate of replacement intersects from below a curve representing the marginal increase in rent thereby obtained. It is only necessary to assume that the latter function is so shaped that one and only one point of intersection from below exists. In the nature of the case this seems highly probable.

In later chapters we will generalize the above analysis by speaking of a single optimum rate of replacement for the entire structure and equipment of a building instead of pointing out repeatedly that each element has its own optimum rate. This generalization is a convenience which does not affect our conclusions.

The solution here proposed does, however, have certain limitations. First of all, it ignores the once-over gains or losses that accrue to the owner in moving from one rate of replacement to another. Suppose that the owner installs a new item at a cost of $100 at a time when demand is such that it will be most profitable for him to replace it every four years at a cost of $25 per year. Now suppose that two years later market demand shifts and the owner calculates that thence forward it will be most profitable to replace the item only every eight years at an annual cost of $12.50. The owner has already accumulated half the cost in the first two years, leaving only $50/6, or $8.33, to be charged in the remaining six years. Over those six years he makes a windfall gain of $6 \times (\$12.50 - \$8.33)$, or $25, which equals the amount of "overcharged" depreciation during the first two years. An analogous windfall loss would occur if the change were from a longer to a shorter period of replacement.

Secondly, the analysis assumes that there is an instantaneous adjustment of rent to changes in the condition of structure as indicated by rate of replacement. This assumption is necessary in order to make the analysis manageable. The introduction of time lags in the response of rent to changes in the rate of replacement would open up the possibility that the owner could earn windfall gains by initiating a lengthening of the period of replacement while demand remains unchanged. Such gains very probably do occur and act as systematic factors affecting market adjustment. But it is not apparent that their introduction would affect our conclusions regarding the influence of taxes. In any event, the present study is limited to what may best be described as comparative statics: the analysis of the condition of rental properties in various states of rest. The costs taken account of for any one state of a building are such as will maintain the building in that state as long as other things remain the same.

Thus far we have discussed the moving of buildings mostly in connection with physical erosion and replacement policy. But movement of the building is also likely to be the owner's response to the three other forms of capital erosion: design obsolescence, market obsolescence, and neighborhood obsolescence. Each of these three involves a downward shift in the demand for the services provided by a given physical structure. The owner will try to improve his economic position by adapting to the new circumstances. He may elect to move his building up or down in the quality scale by varying L and OC, or he may decide to adapt by remodeling.

What are the criteria of profitability for remodeling? The owner will find it worth while to remodel a building if the additional present value so created equals or exceeds the cost of remodeling. Past commitments of capital in the building, being sunk costs, are irrelevant to this calculation. All that matters is the return expected on the additional funds needed to remodel.[14]

To sum up the argument of this chapter, the quality of rental housing depends principally upon three factors:

1. The layout and spaciousness of the apartment units in a structure and the kind and extent of equipment installed in it. These elements depend upon the original cost per room of building and equipping the structure and the subsequent investment in remodeling, if any. They may be summed up under the title "quality of structure." [15]

[14] Ratcliff, *Real Estate Analysis,* pp. 130–31.

[15] An alternative would be to measure quality of structure by the same costs per cubic or per square foot of space, a method that would eliminate the space dimension completely and leave a pure measure of the quality of the space. We will nevertheless use the per-room measure for several reasons. First, when we analyze the demand for "space" in Chapter 3, it will be necessary

2. The level of quality at which the given elements of structure and equipment are maintained, a level which varies with the average rate of replacement $(1/L)$. This factor will sometimes be referred to as "condition of structure."

3. Finally, the level of the annual operating outlays applied to the given structure. For convenience, this element is sometimes referred to as "quality of operation."

It is to these three elements of quality that we will look in later chapters when analyzing the effects of alternative real estate taxes on the maintenance and rehabilitation of rental housing.

---

to use rooms as the unit of space, since that is the only way that housing data are usually available. Second, by using the room as the standard unit of space, we convert size of room into an element of quality, which is probably how most consumers think of it. Third, in the conventional usage of housing analysts, rent and cost comparisons between buildings are made on a per-room basis. Commercial and industrial rentals but not housing rentals are commonly compared in terms of square feet.

CHAPTER THREE

SUPPLY AND DEMAND

In order to focus attention on quality as a variable in the rental housing market, we shall make several simplifying assumptions concerning the supply of factors to the rental housing industry and the behavior of income and prices. These assumptions do not significantly narrow the range of application of our conclusions. The assumptions and some of their consequences are as follows:

1. There is no business cycle and no secular change in price or cost levels, so that the only possible change in income is a secular change in its real level.

2. Factor supplies (including the supply of capital) to the rental housing industry are infinitely elastic, so that (a) new rental units are built whenever the prospective rate of return on them equals or exceeds that for investment generally and ceases whenever it falls below that level and (b) individual operating services are supplied whenever the added rent they are expected to produce equals or exceeds their cost and cease to be supplied when the rent falls below that level.

3. Both the construction industry and the rental housing industry operate at constant cost, so that (a) the expense of building a new structure or remodeling an old one is not affected by the volume of construction activity and (b) the cost of supplying specific operating services is not affected by the volume supplied by the industry.

When we analyzed "The House-Operating Firm" in Chapter 2, we found it unnecessary to treat the demand for quality in rental housing in much detail. It was sufficient to point out that for any single building higher levels of quality of operation would command higher gross rents. We cannot, however, go on to analyze industrywide adjustments in quality without first discussing the nature of market demand for rental housing.

Suppose the operator of a single building improves the quality of his property. He will be able to raise his gross rents not only because some of his original tenants will be willing to pay more rent for the higher quality but also because he will now be able to compete for tenants with other building operators already established at the higher quality, higher rent level.[1] In fact, it is possible for the entire increase in his gross rent to be accounted for by tenants brought in from other high-quality buildings. But when all building operators improve the quality of their properties simultaneously, they cannot, on the average, achieve higher gross rents by attracting tenants from one another. Overall rents can then increase only by the competition of rental housing with home-ownership or with other consumer goods for which it substitutes.

The revenue-cost curve of Chapter 2 describes the relationship between gross rent and costs for single-firm changes only. What can we say about the relationship between revenue and cost when the quality of all rental units in the market changes simultaneously in the same direction? It is precisely such industrywide reactions that we would expect to occur under the impact of changes in the real estate tax system.

Since single firms taken together cannot on balance gain tenants from one another, it is apparent that the response of a single firm's revenue to a change in quality must be weaker when all firms change quality simultaneously than when only the single firm does so. This is analogous to the argument concerning "group equilibrium" under monopolistic competition, in which Chamberlin distinguishes two demand curves for the firm, one for single-firm changes in price, the other—and

[1] See the discussion of the rental-housing industry in Chapter 4 of this book.

much less elastic one—for changes in price by all members of the group simultaneously.[2]

A revenue-cost curve to the house-operating firm for industry-wide changes in quality cannot be precisely defined on a priori grounds. All we can say is that if all firms simultaneously improve quality of operation, gross rent for the industry as a whole will increase but by a smaller proportion than would the revenues of a single firm if it alone made the given improvement in quality. The gross rent received by the industry will increase because as its quality improves, rental housing becomes more attractive relative to other consumer goods with which it competes, including owner-occupied housing. For the additional amenities implied in higher quality, consumers will be prepared to add an increment to their total rent outlay.

The demand for housing consists of two analytically distinct elements: the demand for space and the demand for quality. (As explained in Chapter 2, note 15, we take the room to be the standard unit of space.) Each consumer buys quality and space according to his own scale of preferences. Ideally, he arranges his expenditures so that the marginal utility of the last dollar spent on space is equal to the marginal utility of the last dollar spent on each other good. Indeed, the rental housing market in a large city permits each consumer to come close to fulfilling such ideal aims, for apartments are available in many sizes within each quality range. Thus, we may think of each consumer as having preferences for space and quality that could be related by the conventional indifference map if we could measure quality cardinally.[3]

One would expect, a priori, that the demand for space would increase with family size and income and decrease with price, while the demand for quality would increase with income and

[2] Edward H. Chamberlin, *The Theory of Monopolistic Competition* (5th ed., Cambridge, Mass., Harvard University Press, 1946), pp. 90–92.

[3] Indifference analysis was first applied to preferences for housing space and quality, so far as the author knows, by Wallace F. Smith, *An Outline Theory of the Housing Market, with Special Reference to Low-Income Housing and Urban Renewal*, Doctoral Dissertation, University of Washington, 1958 (unpublished), p. 68.

decrease with price and family size. More generally, space would seem to be a necessity, quality a luxury.[4]

Louis Winnick's study of the demand for space indicates that the consumption of space per person does, indeed, rise with income, although much less than proportionately. More precisely, he finds that average household size increases with income; average number of rooms rented increases faster than average household size but not so fast as income, so that the persons-per-room ratio for renters, after rising from 0.77 in the income class under $1,000 to 0.89 in the $1,000-to-$1,999 class, falls steadily to 0.75 in the $7,000-to-$9,999 class and to 0.66 in the $10,000-and-over category.[5]

When we compare the above data with various estimates of the income elasticity of demand for housing, it becomes clear that increased consumption of space accounts for only a minor fraction of the increase in housing expenditure that accompanies a rise in household income; therefore, the major share of the increase is accounted for by a rise in the quality of space consumed. In fact, the rise in demand for quality as income rises emerges as a major force shaping the demand for and eventually the quality of American housing.

The same point is made explicitly in a work completed more recently than Winnick's, though, like his, based largely on data from the 1950 Census of Housing. In her recent extremely comprehensive study, Margaret Reid writes,

For several decades high quality housing appears to have been an important feature distinguishing the consumption of the rich from that of the poor. Housing improves markedly as one goes up the economic hierarchy of consumers—much more than does food and clothing and probably even more than automobiles . . . with housing as with food, increase in quality rather than sheer quantity accounts for most of the rise in consumption with normal income.[6]

These statements are based on her finding that "the elasticity of rooms per person with respect to normal income appears to

---

[4] *Ibid.*, p. 74.

[5] *American Housing and Its Use: The Demand for Shelter Space* (New York, Wiley, 1957), Table 9, p. 27.

[6] *Housing and Income* (Chicago, University of Chicago Press, 1962), pp. 377–78.

be around 0.5," while other portions of her study "imply a coefficient of elasticity of value or rent of housing with respect to normal income between 1.5 and 2.0." [7]

Estimates of the income elasticity of demand for housing vary widely. Schwabe's Law, enunciated in the nineteenth century, held that as family income increased, the proportion going for rent declined. The hypothesis that the income elasticity of demand for housing is positive but less than unity has been supported by the results of numerous statistical studies employing current income as the independent variable.[8] Most recently Maisel and Winnick found an income elasticity of 0.605, using 1950 income and expenditure data.[9] On the other hand, analysts who have made use of Friedman's permanent-income hypothesis, Richard Muth or Margaret Reid, for example, have found higher income elasticities of demand for housing.[10] Comparisons between these varying estimates need not concern us here. What is important is that whether one uses current income or permanent income, as household income rises, a major share of the increase in housing expenditure is accounted for by rising quality, a minor share by greater consumption of space.

The price elasticity of demand for housing, like its income elasticity, has been a subject of much debate. Dusenberry and Kistin estimated it to be only − 0.08. Muth arrived at a much higher estimate, − 0.904.[11] Miss Reid confirmed Muth's finding with her independent conclusion that "several sets of tendencies imply that the price elasticity of housing tends to be around − 1.0, some representing direct and some indirect measurement." [12]

---

[7] *Ibid.*, pp. 378 and 376.   [8] *Ibid.*, pp. 1–2.

[9] Sherman Maisel and Louis Winnick, "Family Housing Expenditures: Elusive Laws and Intrusive Variances," in Conference on Consumption and Savings, University of Pennsylvania, *Proceedings,* ed. by I. Friend and R. Jones (Philadelphia, Consumer Expenditure Study, 1960), I, 373, and Table 4, pp. 374–75.

[10] Reid, *Housing and Income,* pp. 376–78. Muth's study, "The Demand for Non-Farm Housing," appeared in Arnold C. Harberger, *The Demand for Durable Goods* (Chicago, University of Chicago Press, 1960).

[11] Muth, in Harberger, ed., *Demand for Durable Goods,* p. 49. The Dusenberry-Kistin finding is cited in *ibid.,* p. 31.

[12] Reid, *Housing and Income.,* p. 381.

Miss Reid also delved into the relationship between housing price and the demand for space (and, by inference, for quality). She found that

The evidence presented points to a price elasticity of demand for rooms around − 0.30 . . . much, much higher than the price elasticity of demand for housing consumption in general. Such difference is not surprising. It seems highly probable that demand for space, as represented by rooms, is quite inelastic, whereas demand for quality of housing is quite elastic.[13]

Thus, we have further evidence that space can be treated as a necessity, quality as a luxury.

The analysis of housing demand into quality and space components suggests a curious possibility. Suppose that a local government were to subsidize quality in rental housing in order to encourage landlords to install desirable amenities in the existing stock. This would, in effect, alter the price of quality relative to the price of space. If there is sufficient substitutability between these components, it is conceivable that renters would give up space in order to obtain higher quality quarters than they had before. As a result, the sum of consumer outlays for rent might actually fall instead of rising as housing quality generally improved, income and population remaining constant. But this possibility is quite remote. It could only occur if the substitution effect in favor of quality and against space were not outweighed by the combined strength of the income effect in favor of both quality and space and the substitution effect in favor of quality as compared with other consumer goods. Such an outcome in fact seems unlikely because, first, the pressure of family size probably makes the substitution effect between housing space and quality quite weak, because, second, the above data show that there *is* an income effect favoring space, and because, third, evidence that housing quality is a consumer luxury suggests that it competes strongly with a large group of consumer nonhousing expenditures. We therefore feel safe in assuming that those taxes or subsidies that lower the

13 *Ibid.*, p. 348.

price of quality will not have the effect of reducing the demand for space, or of lowering industrywide gross rent.

An increase in the demand for rental housing could evidently involve either an increase in the demand for space or an increase in the demand for quality or a combination of both. We will find it useful in later chapters to distinguish two possible causes of an increase in the demand for housing. First, income per household might increase as a result of the secular growth of the economy, while number and average size of households remained constant. Second, number of households might increase, while average size and income per household and relative distribution of households by size of income remained constant.[14] For convenience, the first case will be referred to as "rising income," the second as "rising population."

Rising population would clearly increase the demand for space. Since we assume that the number of households would increase by the same proportion at all income levels, all rental housing firms would find their revenue-cost curves rising, for the new households, by competing for space, would drive rent per unit of space up. What would be the effect on demand for quality? The new households can be assumed to have the same taste for quality as those already in being. From that side there would be no change in the demand for quality. We must, however, allow for income and substitution effects on the de-

[14] The way in which a rise in per capita income affects housing demand by rental class has been analyzed in detail in Chester Rapkin, Louis Winnick, and David M. Blank, *Housing Market Analysis* (Washington, D.C., Housing and Home Finance Agency, 1953), Chap. VII, and in Sherman J. Maisel, *An Approach to the Problem of Analysing Housing Demand,* Doctoral Dissertation, Harvard University, 1948 (unpublished), Chap. VII (using current income to establish rent-income relationships). In Chap. VI, the latter analyzes the effect of demographic changes on housing demand. Herbert W. Robinson also investigates the effects of population change on housing demand, *The Economics of Building* (London, P. S. King, 1939), Chap. III, and of other factors including income, in Chap. IV.

None of the above works, however, draws the distinction here made between demand for space and demand for quality. The first two seek ways of predicting the demand for housing at various rent levels. The last attempts to explain the level of building activity in a dynamic setting. In no case is quality, as a variable element in the output of the house-operating firm discussed, nor is the quality of the standing stock as a whole treated explicitly.

mand for quality as the price of space rises. As we have already explained, the former is likely to be fairly strong and the latter quite weak. We will therefore assume that the effect of a rise in the price of space would be slightly to reduce the demand for quality. Landlords would find that the differentials tenants would be willing to pay for differences in service would be smaller than before. Revenue-cost curves would therefore be slightly flatter on account of the reduced demand for quality but at a considerably higher level, on account of the increased demand for space.

On our assumptions concerning the supply of housing, higher rent would raise profits and induce new construction until rents were reduced once more to a level just sufficient to maintain normal returns. But if some force—say a newly imposed real estate tax—were assumed to inhibit new construction, the effect of a population increase would be to raise each firm's revenue-cost curve and slightly decrease its slope. This change in slope would induce landlords to move leftward along their revenue-cost curves, since the optimum operating point (unitary slope of the curve) would have moved slightly to the left.

Next, consider the case where incomes rise but population remains constant. We have shown above that a rise in household income typically leads to a moderate rise in the demand for space and a more pronounced rise in the demand for quality. The effect of the latter is to make revenue-cost curves steeper. As their income rises, tenants develop an increased taste for quality; they are willing to pay more than formerly for the amenities which define higher qualities of service. Hence, the landlord finds that the differentials he can obtain for specific services are larger than they were, which means that his revenue-cost curve has become steeper. Landlords will therefore be induced to move rightward along their revenue-cost curves toward higher quality of operation. Firms will not, however, move so far right as one might suppose from looking at the revenue-cost curve of the single building, for, as we have already argued, when all firms raise quality simultaneously, the increase in rent obtainable by each is less than when a single firm does so.

In addition to increasing the slope of each firm's curve, a general rise in household income will also increase the demand for space, thus shifting at least some of the curves upward in a parallel sense. As pointed out above, this rise in the price of space would probably have a slight adverse effect on the demand for quality, which would offset somewhat the direct increase in the demand for quality that accompanies rising income.

Analysis of real estate taxes inevitably involves a discussion of the rent of land, a discussion, therefore, of the supply of land and the demand for its services. The supply of urban land we shall assume to be perfectly inelastic in each urban market. This means we ignore such matters as the creation of additional urban sites by draining, filling, or grading. Because the supply of land is perfectly inelastic, the return to land is a pure rent. The amount of such rent is determined jointly by the perfectly inelastic supply on the one hand and the demand for the use of sites on the other, the demand having, we assume, a finite but unknown elasticity. The demand for urban land is derived from the demand for various uses, of which housing is only one. We assume that the number of landowners and the number of potential users is sufficiently large to constitute a competitive market for land.

By "site value" we mean the value of a parcel when it is cleared of all improvements. Thus, the cost of clearing a site of existing unwanted improvements does not affect site value. The site value of any one parcel is affected by the nature of improvements on other related sites but by definition is independent of the nature of the improvement that happens to exist on the particular site.[15]

When, in a later chapter, we come to analyze the effects of various taxes levied on the combined rent or combined value of land and improvements, one of the questions we will have to

15 A notable dissenter to this view is Ernest M. Fisher, who argues that the value of the site and the value of improvements thereon cannot be disentangled even theoretically, let alone in practice. He presents his argument in Ernest M. Fisher and Robert M. Fisher, *Urban Real Estate* (New York, Holt, 1954), pp. 54–57.

answer is, how is the burden of these taxes divided between land and improvements? Indeed, this question is one of the classic puzzles in the history of tax theory. As Herbert A. Simon has shown, the answer cannot be found a priori, since it depends upon two matters that require empirical investigation. First, what is the elasticity of the demand for improvements from which the demand for land use is derived? Second, what is the nature of the relation between demand for land at one place, say the urban center, and at others, say the periphery? [16]

The relationship between rents at various locations is outside the scope of this study. Yet we cannot proceed without a hypothetical solution to the tax puzzle. From among the many possible solutions based upon various assumptions as to the elasticity of demand for improvements and the spatial patterns of such demand, we have chosen two and will examine the consequences of both on each occasion that it becomes necessary to speak of the division of the incidence of a tax as between land and improvements. The first of these solutions is the "classical answer" endorsed, for example, by N. G. Pierson and Alfred Marshall and summed up by Simon in the statement, "A tax on total value or gross rental will be shared by landowner and occupier in the ratio of site rent to building rent." [17] Or, to quote Marshall,

If a uniform Imperial tax be levied on the annual value of all land and buildings, the building part of it tends to settle on the occupier; or on his customers, if he uses the building for trade purposes; but the site part of it tends to settle on the owner for the time being, that is, on the interim owner, in so far as it is imposed during his lease; and on the ultimate owner when he comes into possession.[18]

16 "The Incidence of a Tax on Urban Real Property," reprinted in Richard A. Musgrave and Carl S. Shoup, eds., *Readings in the Economics of Taxation* (Homewood, Ill., Richard D. Irwin, 1959), pp. 416–35.

17 *Ibid.*, p. 424.

18 "Memorandum on the Classification and Incidence of Imperial and Local Taxes," reprinted in *Official Papers by Alfred Marshall* (London, Macmillan, 1926), p. 345.

Simon has shown that this classical answer (Simon's case No. 4) depends upon making two assumptions: first, the demand for accommodation is highly inelastic; second, the difference in site rent between one place and another arises from a difference in transportation costs to the urban center. From these assumptions it follows that

the difference in the respective prices paid for housing on two different sites cannot be affected by a tax. This difference is the rent paid for site. Hence to determine the incidence of a tax we have only to calculate the total tax on a marginal house and on a super-marginal house. Each occupier will bear a tax equal to that on the marginal site [sic], while any excess in tax paid on a super-marginal house will be borne by the site owner.[19]

To this solution F. Y. Edgeworth objected. He denied that the ratio of ground rent to total gross rent has any bearing upon the ratio in which the burden of a tax on the latter is divided between landowner and occupant:

There is no objection to speaking of the "portion which is tax on ground rent," if we are careful to remember that this portion and its proportion to the tax on gross rent has no relation whatever to the amount by which the ground rent tends to be reduced in consequence of the impost.[20]

Edgeworth specifically rejected Pierson's assumption that the house rent paid at the center cannot exceed that paid at the outskirts by more than the cost of transportation from periphery to center.[21] He explored many other possible outcomes and concluded that in the long run the incidence of the tax "will be divided in uncertain proportions" between landowner and tenant.[22] This means that ground landlords might bear either less or more than the proportion of the tax equal to the ratio

[19] In Musgrave and Shoup, *Economics of Taxation*, p. 424. "House" evidently should be substituted for "site" following the word "marginal" in the last sentence.

[20] "Urban Rates," reprinted in his *Papers Relating to Political Economy* (London, Macmillan, 1925), II, 172.

[21] "Answers to Questions Put by the Local Tax Commission," in *ibid.*, p. 136n.

[22] "The Pure Theory of Taxation," in *ibid.*, p. 82.

of site rent to total rent. We may add, however, that the greater the elasticity of demand for accommodation, the more a tax on house rent will reduce the demand for sites and the greater will be the decline in site rent. In view of the evidence already cited that the price elasticity of demand for housing may be close to unity, we have chosen as our second possible solution to the tax puzzle the hypothesis that when a tax is levied on the combined value of land and improvements, the landowner will bear not only the share of the tax attributable to land value (the classical answer) but a part of that attributable to building value as well (Simon's case No. 3).

CHAPTER FOUR

THE
RENTAL–HOUSING
INDUSTRY

The rental-housing industry in a large city is best analyzed as an instance of monopolistic competition among a large group of sellers. Differentiation of the product, the large number of firms, and the small size of the largest in relation to the whole market make this a good case for Chamberlin's large-group solution.[1] Differentiation follows inevitably from the very nature of the taste for housing and the distribution of income. We know that as consumers' incomes rise, they typically demand not only more space but space of higher quality. Since incomes are not distributed uniformly among families, it follows that there will always be a demand for rental units not only of various sizes but also of various qualities. To take the extreme case, suppose we start with a rental housing market consisting of 100 identical structures, containing identical units maintained at a uniform level of quality. Even if we rule out new construction or remodeling, it is impossible to suppose that these 100 structures will long remain uniform. Over time they will gradually become differentiated as some owners find it profitable to dress their property up to appeal to expensive

[1] Edward H. Chamberlin, *The Theory of Monopolistic Competition* (5th ed., Cambridge, Mass., Harvard University Press, 1946), pp. 81–100. Chester Rapkin, Louis Winnick, and David M. Blank, *Housing Market Analysis* (Washington, D.C., Housing and Home Finance Agency, 1953), p. 22, also note the resemblance to "monopolistic competition in conventional economic analysis."

tastes and others allow it to slip to a level of quality and cost appropriate to the lower income groups in the market. It would be much more convenient if we could analyze the effects of taxes on housing quality in a market model in which all structures were always identical in quality, but our observations concerning taste and distribution of income coupled with reasonable assumptions about the profit-seeking behavior of building owners forbid us to construct any such model. We must accept differentiation as inevitable.[2]

Our model also conforms with Chamberlin's large-group solution in that we assume we are dealing with an urban rental-housing market in which the number of sellers is sufficiently large "to render each member of it a negligible influence upon the others."[3] By this assumption we avoid all problems of strategy: each building operator behaves as though his own acts did not affect any of his competitors. Although we shall not attempt to confirm the point statistically, there can be little doubt that most rental-housing units in the United States are found in markets large enough to conform with the conditions for a large-group solution.

One might go farther and classify all rental-housing structures in each market into a half-dozen large groups according to the rent range served by each building. The dividing lines in any such system of large groups, however, are necessarily arbitrary; hence, for most analytical purposes we shall not employ it. Robert Triffin carried the analysis of the effects of product differentiation on market structure to its logical end and found that the concept of "industry" vanished into the air, leaving behind the notion of a continuous web of competing

[2] Most consumer goods are subject to the same inevitable differentiation as to quality. But quality as a variable is not often discussed systematically, perhaps because it is not considered to have much social significance. Among the sources consulted, only Smith deals with housing quality itself. His treatment differs from that employed here in numerous respects. He does not, of course, deal with the effect of taxes on quality. Wallace F. Smith, *An Outline Theory of the Housing Market, with Special Reference to Low-Income Housing and Urban Renewal*, Doctoral Dissertation, University of Washington, 1958 (unpublished).

[3] Chamberlin, *Monopolistic Competition*, p. 100.

firms.[4] Logically, the rental-housing market, taken in isolation, is itself such a continuous web. Nevertheless, since our problems require us to study relationships among different grades of housing, we shall have to resort to the concept of competing large groups of housing units, however arbitrary may be the points of division between them.

The quality of housing service provided in a given structure we have thus far measured in terms of total cost or total rent for the firm, but in order to compare quality as between buildings and discuss the industry as a whole, we need standards of measure that are independent of the size of the structure. The required measures are cost and rent per room. (See Chapter 2, note 15.) The rental housing market can then be thought of as a distribution of rentable space by rent or cost per room. (Whether rent or cost is the better measure and the relationships between these two will be discussed later.) Tenants will choose their quarters according to their taste, income, and family size, with, of course, a tendency for the rich to live in high-rent buildings and the poor in low.

Since each existing structure contains a given number of rooms, reducing the rent and cost concepts developed in preceding chapters to a per-room basis in no way alters the relationships between them for each building and requires no special explanation.

Graphically, the rental-housing market in a given metropolitan area can be pictured as a series of revenue-cost curves (per-room basis) such as those shown in Figure 4.1. For convenience we may assume that each of the five R/C curves represents a large number of identical structures in a given rent-cost bracket. Faced by given tastes, population, and income distribution in the local market, profit-maximizing building owners will attempt to "move" their buildings by the processes described in Chapter 2 to the most profitable rent bracket attainable, given the location and structure of their

4 *Monopolistic Competition and General Equilibrium Theory* (Cambridge, Mass., Harvard University Press, 1940).

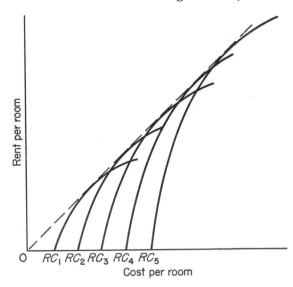

FIGURE 4.1   THE RENTAL-HOUSING INDUSTRY

buildings, the code constraints, and so on. This move will be accomplished by remodeling if necessary, by choosing the appropriate rate at which to replace structure, and by finding the optimum quality of operation for the structure.

If we assume free entry of new firms, then when the rental-housing market is in equilibrium, all firms will be (1) earning normal profits and (2) operating at a point of tangency between their R/C curve and the diagonal. (3) There will be no possibility of earning supernormal profits through further moves of existing buildings.

Assuming that there are no cyclical shifts in income and prices, equilibrium in the rental-housing industry may still be disturbed by such forces as changes in population, secular changes in the level or distribution of income, changes in technology and design, or changes in the location of economic activity. If any such noncyclical change, which is expected to persist, be imagined to disturb the market, how would equilibrium be restored? If an active response by building owners is possible and profitable, they will seek to move their buildings by remodeling, by changes in the rate of replacement of structure, and/or by changes in quality of operation. If new construction is possible at the relevant rent levels, that, too, will help to restore equilibrium. To the extent that neither moving nor new construction restores normal returns to all owners, we are left with residual departures from the norm which will be removed in the following ways:

1. If the departure is due to the rise or fall in popularity of a particular neighborhood or location, the rise or fall in total rent will be attributable to location alone and will eventually lead to a rise or fall in land rent at that location. Since land rent is a part of total annual cost of the building owner, his rate of return will in the long run be restored to normal by this means.

2. If the departure is due to any cause not associated with location and not adjustable by moving or the competition of new construction, then the market adjusts by capitalizing the expected departure into the market, or capital value of the property. By definition, this means that a normal rate of return is restored.

Since full equilibrium of the market requires normal returns and tangency for all firms, it necessarily means that total annual rent equals total annual cost for every structure. Thus, in equilibrium it makes no difference whether quality of housing is measured by rent or cost. Inputs, measured by cost, provide the services; consumer expenditure, measured by rent, evaluates them. In equilibrium, under the competitive assumptions we make, the two are always equal. When the market is not in equilibrium, some building owners may be earning positive or negative quasi-rents, which enter as a wedge between total rent and total cost as here defined.

CHAPTER FIVE

A DIGRESSION CONCERNING SLUMS

Our analysis up to this point reveals three dimensions to the problem of housing standards and therefore to the problem of slums: first, the quality of the structure—a function of original construction cost and subsequent outlays for remodeling; second, the condition of structure—a function of outlays for replacement; third, the level of quality of operation—a function of variable operating costs. However, the problem is not nearly that simple. There is another significant dimension, which is summed up under the heading of occupancy. Occupancy lends itself to two further distinctions: the quantity of occupancy and the quality of the occupants. A fine building can easily be made into a slum by converting it to single-room occupancy and putting a large family in each room.[1] Likewise, an ordinary tenement may be classed as respectable housing if the tenants are all well-behaved and socially responsible, whereas the same structure becomes a slum if occupied largely by brawling and destructive problem families. Inevitably, the analysis of occupancy carries one into urban sociology. Housing analysts therefore frequently deal with the question of who lives in the slums or in slum-clearance projects and how the social character-

[1] Webster defines a slum as "A thickly-populated street or alley esp. one marked by squalor, wretched living conditions, or the degradation of its inhabitants." We take the liberty, now common enough, of applying the term to single buildings as well. *Webster's New International Dictionary* (2d ed., Springfield, Mass., Merriam, 1961).

istics and organization of this population have been changing.[2] Although such studies would be of great importance in an exhaustive analysis of the slum problem, they will not be reviewed here, where a deliberate attempt is being made to focus on economic processes.

Basically, the concept of the "slum" is subjective. Each observer draws his own picture of minimum standard housing, and whatever falls below the standard is a slum. There is, of course, a social standard of adequacy implied in the building, occupancy, and sanitary codes of our large cities. These codes do typically have something to say about all four dimensions of the slum problem. But most observers would probably agree that, even if the present codes were enforced, they would not set a high enough standard to eliminate slums.

Although it is impossible to define a slum precisely, a division of the problem into its four elements at least allows us to think about the matter with greater precision. In particular, it helps us to avoid holding inconsistent views on the various aspects of the slum problem.

To illustrate, let us suppose that we can measure cardinally the quality of housing services provided by each rental housing structure. Assume that we have a scale of quality running from 1 to 100 and that we lay this out horizontally in a diagram. (See Figure 5.1.)

At this point we wish to abstract from problems of occupancy, so we shall assume that all families are equally clean, orderly, and responsible and that overcrowding (however defined) is effectively prohibited by law. In that case the quality of the services provided by any given building depends upon the remaining three elements of the slum problem, as we have defined it: quality of structure, condition of structure, and quality of operation.

2 For example, see Elizabeth Wood, *The Small Hard Core: The Housing of Problem Families in New York City* (New York, Citizen's Housing and Planning Council of New York, 1957); and John R. Seeley, "The Slum: Its Nature, Use, and Users," *Journal of the American Institute of Planners*, February, 1959, pp. 7–14.

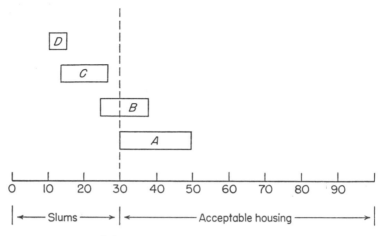

FIGURE 5.1   SLUMS VS. ACCEPTABLE HOUSING

The owner can move his building up or down in the rent distribution by varying these elements. The first—the nature (or lavishness) of the structure—determines the particular sector on the quality scale at which the building is found. The second and third provide a range of quality of service attainable with a particular building. Let us first assume that the owner holds the quality and condition of structure fixed and varies only his operating outlays.

Then building *A* is located in the neighborhood of output quality 40. The actual output of the building may vary from 30 to 50, depending upon how the building is operated. The lower limit of 30 is set by the existence of housing and sanitary codes: if *A* is a relatively good building, then no matter how badly it is operated, if the basic services required by law are kept up, the quality of the building as a residence cannot sink to zero. Moreover, the lower limit for a relatively good building such as *A* must be above that for a relatively poor one such as *C*, since at the limit both provide the legally required minimum services, but *A* retains the advantage of, for example, the more spacious layouts that were built into its original structure.

The upper limit of 50 for building *A* is set by the fact that with a given structure there is a limit to the quality of service which it is practical to obtain by increased outlays on operation.

Somewhere on the scale of quality in Figure 5.1 each of us places his dividing line between slums and acceptable housing. Suppose that it is at quality 30. Then building *B* straddles the divide: if it is well-run, it is acceptable; if ill-run, it becomes a slum. Building *C*, on the other hand, remains a slum no matter how it is operated—but it can range from rather poor to almost acceptable in quality. Finally, building *D* is far down in the scale of slums and offers little scope for improvement through better operation.

This schematic exercise shows that whether or not quality of operation is an important dimension of the slum problem depends upon how much scope there is for improved quality of service from existing buildings. If all buildings resemble *D*, then quality of operation is but a minor aspect of the slum problem, but if many of them resemble *A, B,* and *C*, it is not to be neglected. This is a matter for empirical investigation.

We have explained in earlier chapters that the owner can move his building from one rental class to another not only in the short run by varying his operating outlays but also, over the long run, by varying his fixed costs. He can move it either by remodeling it or by increasing or decreasing the average period over which he replaces structural parts and equipment. Thus, if we allow owners to vary structure as well as operating outlays, the "quality boxes," which appear fixed in Figure 5.1, themselves become movable in response to changing market conditions. Such moves are undoubtedly significant in adapting a given stock of housing to changing patterns of demand. How significant they might be in improving the standard of housing for the poor is again a matter for empirical investigation.[3]

---

[3] One recent empirical study of rehabilitation is William W. Nash, *Residential Rehabilitation: Private Profits and Public Purposes* (New York, McGraw-Hill, 1959). Projects now going forward in many cities will soon add important data on the costs and returns to be expected from publicly aided rehabilitation.

On the whole, we lay too much of the blame for slums on slum owners. To be sure, the slum landlords' sins are often real enough. The owner whose properties accumulate dozens of violations, who cannot be found for service of a summons, and who pays his fines when at last brought to account but immediately begins to flout the codes again has been revealed and re-revealed in an endless series of newspaper exposés. Yet despite his own guilt, there is a sense in which he is only a scapegoat: he lives off the slums but he has not caused them—poor housing is essentially the product of poverty.

If we wish to eliminate housing below some socially established minimum quality level, there are only a few ways we might do it. One is to eliminate poverty. A second is to replace all slums with public housing or with subsidized private housing. A third is to enforce code standards at a sufficiently high level. But the first way is not yet feasible and the second is too expensive for most tastes. The third is a matter of degree and up to a point is already in operation. But tightening codes to the point where they would eliminate all of what are usually called slums would probably involve far more compulsion than we would (or probably should) tolerate. It is too easily forgotten that in a housing market with a normal vacancy rate at all quality levels, the enforcement of housing codes may involve compulsion of buyers as well as sellers, for we may then infer that tenants who live in substandard quarters (if they are not victims of discrimination) do so out of economic choice and that landlords would provide more amenities or better housing if tenants were willing or able to pay for them. The case is even clearer with regard to density of occupancy: when we tell a poor family that they may not legally live five in one room, we are forcing them to rent two rooms. That may, in turn, create an obligation upon society to pay the added rent, so that in the end higher code standards, too, have a price on them, and if it is proposed to raise standards appreciably, the price may be high.

In fact, we have moved gradually along all three routes

toward the elimination of slums, but the knowledge that progress has been and is likely to remain slow ought to encourage us
to investigate the impact of real estate taxes on housing standards and to consider whether any conceivable tax reform would
speed our progress by freeing or encouraging the movement of
existing buildings toward higher standards of quality.

CHAPTER SIX

VARIETIES
OF THE LOCAL
REAL ESTATE TAXES

The alternative real estate tax systems whose effects we wish to examine may be defined as follows:

Tax Type	Brief Definition
No. 1	An ad valorem tax on assessed site value.
No. 2	An ad valorem tax on the assessed value of site and improvements combined.
No. 3	A proportional tax on the actual gross rent of site and improvements combined.
No. 4	A tax on the net income from site and improvements combined.
No. 5	A tax along the lines of the British "rates."
No. 6	Any of the above combined with various forms of tax abatement to encourage maintenance and rehabilitation.
No. 7	Any of the above combined with tax penalties to encourage maintenance and rehabilitation.

In the United States the real estate tax is typically a local charge, levied by cities, towns, counties, school districts, and other local taxing units under authority derived from state laws.[1] In most states, the tax on real property is only a part—

[1] The standard descriptive work has long been Jens P. Jensen, *Property Taxation in the United States* (Chicago, University of Chicago Press, 1931). It contains an extensive, though now long out-of-date bibliography.

Dick Netzer's volume, *Economics of the Property Tax* (Washington, D.C..

although by far the major part—of a more or less general property tax. The manner in which real estate taxes are levied is prescribed by law in each state. Among the fifty states legal and administrative differences, of course, abound. For our purposes, however, most of these are irrelevant. Much more important is the fact that with few exceptions United States real estate is taxed by means of an ad valorem levy on the assessed value of site and improvements combined—tax No. 2 in our list of types.

The long history of real estate taxation in the United States has brought with it an almost equally long history of criticisms of the tax and proposals for its reform. Few of the proposals for using a tax base other than combined assessed value of site and improvements have been tested for periods long enough or over areas wide enough to yield much evidence on their effects. Our list of tax types includes, however, most of those that seem interesting and even remotely feasible. We have confined the list to variations on the *local* real estate tax.

Next we must describe our tax types in a manner that will permit us to depict them on revenue-cost diagrams of the kind developed in Chapters 2 and 4. To facilitate comparison, we have drawn some of the tax diagrams in such a manner that at the moment of impact, before the firm has adjusted to them, all the tax types depicted would produce identical revenues from the firm in question. Our ultimate purpose, of course, is to see what kinds of quality adjustment both the firm and the industry might be expected to make to the various tax types. We shall therefore wish to compare, if possible (and in some cases it may not be possible), the effects of each tax with every other *after* full adjustment has taken place. One would like to add, "and with revenues, after full adjustment, equal for all tax types." But our model is incapable of specifying the final tax yield in all cases. Our ultimate answers will therefore be given

---

The Brookings Institution, 1966) promises to be the indispensable descriptive and analytical work on the subject for some years to come. It was, however, still in preparation when this study was completed.

in terms of differential incidence upon quality of taxes which yield equal revenues at the time they are imposed. The first description of and comparison among the taxes, however, is most easily accomplished by examining the situation before the firms adjust quality to the tax.

Let it be assumed that before the taxes are imposed, the firms and the industry are in full equilibrium. As explained in Chapter 4, this means that all firms are earning normal profits and are at the optimum level of quality of operation and no unexploited possibilities for earning supernormal profits by "moving" remain. It will then be possible to show a real estate tax diagramatically as a modification of each firm's revenue-cost curve. The revenue-cost curve is a locus of attainable short-run operating positions. Thus, the diagrams will show initially only the short-run impact of each tax. Analysis of the long-run impact, via effects on investment, will be held for Chapter 8.

Tax No. 1

Tax No. 1 is an ad valorem tax on the assessed value of site only. Since site value is independent of the value or condition of improvements that happen to exist on the site, an ad valorem tax on site value may for our purpose be depicted as a fixed tax, constant for all levels of operating outlay and all levels of replacement outlay on any given structure. Such a fixed tax can be represented either as a constant element in fixed cost or as a constant absolute deduction from gross rent at all levels of rent. We shall use the latter procedure in order to retain the cost scale as a visually unambiguous ordinal scale of quality. Thus, in Figure 6.1 the revenue-cost curve before tax is shown by the line RC. By deducting a fixed tax from gross rent, we derive a revenue-cost curve after tax. For the sake of brevity we shall call this the net revenue-cost curve, or net RC_1 (the subscript numeral indicates the tax type). Net RC_1 is a vertical displacement of the revenue-cost curve and thus preserves the latter's slope at each cost point.

Tax No. 1 is the levy advocated by those who favor untaxing

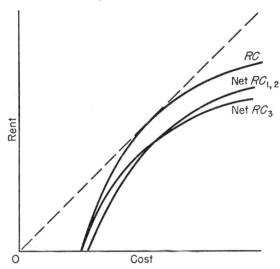

FIGURE 6.1   TAXES NO. 1, NO. 2, AND NO. 3

improvements but retaining the tax on land. Advocates of tax
No. 1 generally would raise the rates sufficiently to extract
from the site-value base alone as much revenue as is now produced by the traditional real estate tax on site and improvements combined.[2]

Tax No. 2

Tax No. 2, the ad valorem tax on the combined assessed
value of land and improvements, is the familiar American real
estate tax. Since assessment is usually done locally, since the
laws under which it is done vary from state to state, and since

---

[2] This is perhaps too strong a statement, since many advocates of heavier
site-value taxation contemplate drastically reducing the tax on improvements
without necessarily eliminating it. Proposals for shifting the whole load of the
real estate tax onto a site-value base are, however, not uncommon. One such
proposal for New York City was submitted as a bill to the New York State
legislature in 1915 and was taken seriously enough to be made the object of a
detailed study by Robert M. Haig entitled *Some Probable Effects of the Exemption of Improvements from Taxation in the City of New York*, a report prepared for the Committee on Taxation of the City of New York (New York, 1915).

the practice of assessors often departs notoriously from what the law requires, we will have to adopt a hypothetical model of this tax which will not always correspond with actual conditions: we shall assume that properties are uniformly assessed at their full market value. (Actually it would do as well to assume that they are uniformly assessed at any given proportion of full market value.)

Market value we have explained as the present value of expected future returns. In order to depict tax No. 2, we have to know how market value varies with operating outlays. We know that present income is maximized when the property is operated at the optimum level of quality. If it is operated either above or below the optimum level, present income is reduced. But does it follow that market value, assessed value, and therefore liability for tax No. 2 is also reduced if the owner moves away from the optimum operating point? The answer is that it does not follow. The tax is based essentially upon the market's estimate of the property's potential earning power. If a particular owner fails to operate the building in the most profitable way, this will not influence the market or the assessor.

Since tax No. 2 will not vary with operating outlays, it can be represented diagramatically as a constant absolute deduction from gross rent. Thus, the same curve that illustrates tax No. 1 can be used to illustrate tax No. 2. (See net RC_1 and net RC_2 in Figure 6.1.) In practice, of course, it would be unlikely that the two taxes would be equal for any one property, even though they produced the same total revenue for the government.

It will be recalled from Chapter 2 that there is no logical dividing line (but only a conventional one) between repairs, which are classified as an operating outlay, and replacement of worn-out structure and equipment, which is classified as an investment. This difficulty now reappears when we assert that tax No. 2 is invariant to changes in operating outlay. What we are here saying is that the market and assessed values of a property will not vary with its state of repair, although they *will* vary with its state of replacement. The relevant attribute of repairs or operating outlays is that they have no capital value. They do not represent stored-up wealth because their expected life is short. (This is not strictly true of some operating outlays—a paint job in the public halls of a building may last five or ten years—but as an approximation the conventional distinction will serve.) Structural parts and equipment, on the other hand, have a relatively long useful life and, if they have not reached the end of it, are a store of value and therefore a fit object for tax No. 2.

The proposition that assessors take no account of the operating condition of a building may seem a bit too strong. Yet it was affirmed in conversation by the Assistant Director of Assessment in the Tax Department of the City of New York.[3] Here is a subject that might be worthy of empirical investigation.

Tax No. 3

Tax No. 3 is a proportional tax on gross rent. This can readily be shown as a constant proportional deduction from gross rent along the whole length of the revenue-cost curve. It is depicted in Figure 6.1 as resulting in net RC_3, a curve whose slope at each cost point is less than the slope of the original revenue-cost curve by a percentage equal to the tax rate.

Tax No. 3 is levied on the gross rent of site and improvement combined. The tax applies to actual rather than assessed gross rent. Therefore, even if (unlike the British "rates") it were collected from the owner rather than the tenant, it would not fall upon vacant property.

Tax No. 4

Tax No. 4 is a tax on the net income from site and improvements combined. Like tax No. 3, it applies to an actual rather than an assessed base. We have adopted the convention of including "normal" profits in the firm's costs. Thus, a firm oper-

[3] Interview with the late Alfred Jacobsen, June 8, 1962.

ating at the point at which its *RC* curve is tangent to the 45-degree diagonal is earning normal profits, although the diagram shows total cost equal to gross rent. In Figure 6.2 the

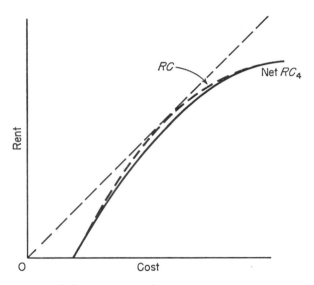

FIGURE 6.2   TAX NO. 4—A TAX ON NET INCOME

dashed curve which rises to tangency with the 45-degree diagonal is the revenue-cost curve of such a firm.

When the housing market is in full equilibrium, it will be possible for the owner of a rental structure to earn normal profits only by operating at the optimum quality level. If he moves to a lower quality level, his gross rents fall off more than his costs, and profits decline; if he moves to a higher quality level, his gross rents do not rise as fast as his costs and, again, profits decline. We assume that the tax on profits is at a constant rate. Hence, the amount of tax paid will rise to a maximum at the optimum quality of operation and fall off again beyond that point. To depict the net revenue-cost curve, net RC_4 (the solid curve in Figure 6.2), we deduct from gross rent the amount of tax paid at each quality of operation, leaving a crescent-shaped space between *RC* and net

RC_4, the height of which shows the amount of tax that would be paid as quality varied.

Since we assume that every property is owned free of debt, the question of the deductibility of interest for tax purposes does not arise.

Tax No. 5

Tax No. 5 is an ad valorem tax along the lines of the United Kingdom's "rates." It is included here not because its adoption has been urged in America but because it provides an interesting and long-established contrast to American practice.

Ralph Turvey describes the British real estate tax in these words:

Rates, as known in the United Kingdom, are an *ad valorem* tax, the tax base being the net annual value of occupied real property. This is the rent that could be obtained by letting a property from year to year *net* of maintenance and insurance expenses. It is thus the net annual rental value of property gross of depreciation.[4]

The statement that the tax base is rent "net of maintenance and insurance" suggests erroneously that we have here a tax on what has sometimes been called the "net free and clear return" from real property. One soon discovers, however, that the allowance for maintenance and insurance is arrived at by a statutory formula and therefore has nothing whatever to do with the actual expenses incurred by the property owner. The tax therefore turns out to be closer to a gross-rent than a net-rent tax.

Briefly, the tax is calculated in the following manner for residential properties in England and Wales. (The tax takes a different form in Scotland and is also somewhat different for nonresidential properties.) The annual rental value of each property is determined by central assessment. From this "assessed gross annual value" there is then deducted an allowance for the annual maintenance and repairs necessary to maintain

[4] *The Economics of Real Property: An Analysis of Property Values and Patterns of Use* (New York, Macmillan, 1957), p. 67.

the building in condition to yield such gross value. The deduction consists, however, not of the actual expenses incurred but of a specific ratio of the gross value. The allowable ratio is established by law. It is not the same for all levels of gross value but decreases in a few steps as the gross value rises. Gross value less the allowable deduction equals "ratable value," which is the tax base. The "rate," as this tax is called, is then levied by each locality on the property within its jurisdiction at a constant percent of ratable value. The tenant, not the landlord, is liable for the tax. Hence, if the property is vacant, no tax is due.[5]

From the description it should be clear that British "rates" are essentially taxes on assessed gross annual rent. Since the allowable deduction from gross value is itself a ratio of gross value, the tax is not a *net* tax in any real sense. Even though it is levied at a fixed rate, the tax is somewhat progressive to gross value because the allowable percentage deduction diminishes as gross value increases.

British "rates," our tax No. 5, are depicted in Figure 6.3. "Assessed gross annual value," which we shall assume equals actual gross rent, is plotted on the vertical scale. *RC* shows this variable plotted against total cost. To arrive at "ratable value," we deduct 40 percent from assessed gross annual value for all points up to the midpoint on our rent axis and 40 percent plus 25 percent of the excess above the midpoint rent for all points beyond that. (The choice of rates and brackets is merely illustrative. The allowable British deductions actually run from 40 percent in the lowest rent bracket through several steps to a marginal rate of one-sixth in the highest rent bracket.) [6] The tax is then levied against ratable value at a hypothetical rate of 20 percent, and the tax liability is deducted vertically from

[5] For a general explanation of valuation for rating, see the *Report of the Commissioners of Her Majesty's Inland Revenue,* for the year ended March, 31, 1961, Cmnd. 1598 (London, H. M. Stationery Office, 1962), pp. 175–79. Practice departs from our brief description in one important respect: residential properties are valued by reference to June, 1939, rather than current rentals (*ibid.,* p. 176).

[6] *Ibid.,* p. 177.

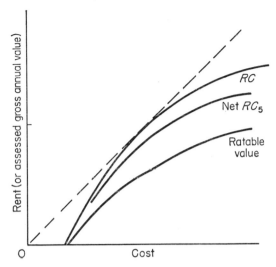

FIGURE 6.3   TAX NO. 5—THE BRITISH "RATES"

the *RC* curve to yield net RC_5 in Figure 6.3. This last step involves the assumption that although the tax is levied on the tenant, it is shifted entirely onto the landlord in the short run (just as soon as expiring leases make it possible for tenants to reduce their rent payments by the amount of the newly imposed tax).

The slope of net RC_5 is less than that of the revenue-cost curve before tax by a percentage equal to the marginal effective tax rate on assessed gross annual value. The marginal effective tax rate rises as rent rises because the allowable percentage deduction diminishes as rent rises. Therefore, the slope of net RC_5 is a decreasing fraction of the slope of the pre-tax revenue-cost curve as rent increases.

Tax No. 6

Tax No. 6 consists of any of our other tax types combined with some form of tax abatement to encourage either improved maintenance or rehabilitation. Since in this chapter we attempt to depict only the short-run impact of taxes, we are concerned with tax No. 6 only in so far as it might stimulate higher operating outlays (that is, a movement *along* the revenue-cost curve to the right rather than any shift of the curve itself). To represent tax No. 6, we have chosen an abatement in the form of an agreement not to raise his tax bill in the event that the owner performs specified desirable acts.

The taxing authority could enter into an agreement with a landlord not to raise his assessments (or other tax base) during some specified term if he undertook certain desirable operating improvements. The effect of such an agreement would be to convert the owner's tax liability at whatever amount it then stood into a constant tax for all levels of quality higher than the one at which he was then operating. Of course, only the tax *base* would be fixed. The *rate* would be the same for this owner as for all others and might rise or fall in the course of time.

Obviously, if the basic tax were invariant to operating conditions, like tax No. 1 or No. 2, then this kind of abatement

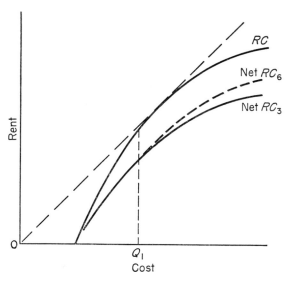

FIGURE 6.4   TAX NO. 6—A TAX ABATEMENT

would have no effect on operating outlays. It would also be without operating effects in the case of a net income tax (tax No. 4), since tax liability is at a maximum, in absolute terms, if the firm is initially in equilibrium; to freeze it at its maximum level cannot encourage the owner to improve his operation.

Such tax abatement would therefore affect operating outlays only in the case of the taxes that increase with rising gross rent, namely, taxes No. 3 and No. 5. In Figure 6.4 we have illustrated this kind of tax abatement as applied to tax No. 3, the gross rent tax. With the gross rent tax in force (net RC_3), the owner finds his optimum operating level to be Q_1. If he is then granted tax abatement for operating improvements, his tax liability remains fixed at the amount due at Q_1, and his new revenue-cost curve for points to the right of Q_1 is net RC_6.

Tax No. 7

Tax No. 7 consists of any of our other types combined with tax penalties to encourage maintenance and rehabilitation. In Figure 6.5 we illustrate tax No. 7. Several technical difficulties must be explained. First, the penalty approach implies the definition by society of some minimum essential bundle of housing services. We must assume that this definition is not such as to cause landlords to change the order in which services are provided as quality is increased, for if they change the order, we cannot use given revenue-cost curves as a starting point for the analysis. What we must, in fact, assume is no more nor less than that the social ranking of services corresponds with that provided by the market. Second, such a social standard can be marked off on the horizontal cost-quality scale of the revenue-cost diagram for each building—but it will not occur at the same rent-cost level in every structure, on account of differences in fixed costs.

Once a minimum standard has been socially defined, any buildings found to be operating to the left of that quality point are subject to a penalty. The penalty, of course, termi-

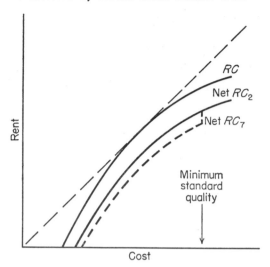

FIGURE 6.5   TAX NO. 7—A TAX PENALTY

nates when services are improved up to the minimum standard, so there will be a discontinuity at that point on the net RC_7 curve (unless some mathematician prevails upon the tax commission to formulate a penalty that disappears asymptotically).

One can conceive of many ways in which a tax penalty might be formulated; most of them, however, would probably be unconstitutional in most states. Probably the only legal way to achieve the desired result would be to insist on full-value assessment of substandard properties. In places where old tenement properties have traditionally been underassessed by comparison with other housing, or where all housing has been assessed at less than full value, there may be considerable leeway within the law for substantially penalizing substandard properties by raising their assessments to the upper limit.

This kind of penalty would involve a constant percentage increase in the tax base in the case of a tax for which the base is an assessed quantity—such as tax No. 2. Since liability for tax No. 2 is itself invariant to operating outlays, the penalty would consist in a constant dollar increase in the amount of tax paid at all levels of quality up to the minimum standard. The penalty can therefore be shown by lowering the left-hand portion of the net RC curve by a constant amount, as we have done in Figure 6.5 (net RC_7).

A penalty could also be attached to a gross-rent tax to raise tax liability by a constant percentage at all quality levels below the minimum standard. But since such a tax is based on actual rather than assessed gross rents, the penalty could only be applied by levying a higher tax rate on some properties than on others, and this would raise legal problems. The same objection would prevent use of a penalty in connection with tax No. 4, the net-income tax.

CHAPTER SEVEN

THE EFFECT OF LOCAL REAL ESTATE TAXES ON OPERATING DECISIONS

In Chapter 2 we argued that the behavior of the house-operating entrepreneur is best explained by analysis of the two kinds of decisions he makes: operating decisions, whose effects work themselves out in the short run, and investment decisions, which require a longer planning period, or time horizon. The effects of alternative real estate taxes on rental housing can best be analyzed by reference to the same twofold classification.

Assume to begin with that the rental-housing industry in a given housing market is in full equilibrium with one of the seven varieties of real estate tax in force. Now suppose the government discards the initial real estate tax and substitutes one of the alternatives. Upon impact, or within a year or two, the tax change will affect the short-run operating decisions of rental-housing firms. In this chapter we shall analyze such short-run, or impact, effects for each of the alternative taxes. In the following chapter we shall analyze the long-run effects of the taxes on remodeling and rate of replacement of structure which would be fully worked out only after a given levy had shaped investment decisions over a period of many years.

The division into short and long run is also useful with respect to tax shifting. In so far as real estate taxes can be shifted from owners to tenants, they are shifted only through effects on investment and hence only in the long run. Therefore, this chapter does not deal with the shifting process but only with what are properly thought of as impact effects. The chapter that follows will build on this one, adding shifting and investment effects onto operating effects to arrive at a final statement. This procedure is justified because of the extent to which the short- and long-run effects of the taxes differ—some of those which are neutral to operating decisions are not neutral to investment decisions.

In both chapters we will deal with a single housing market which is assumed to fall entirely within one taxing jurisdiction. Within the jurisdiction, taxes are imposed uniformly. Moreover, the selected housing market is treated as though it were isolated from all other housing markets and taxing jurisdictions, so that we need not consider the effects of tax competition.

One cannot treat a change in the real estate tax system as though it were a marginal adjustment requiring no more than the usual partial equilibrium analysis of the incidence of an excise. If a tax with so copious a yield is to be newly imposed, one must take into account the resulting change in expenditures. As Ralph Turvey has pointed out, the neoclassical writers met this difficulty by drawing

their distinction between onerous and beneficial rates, the latter being those which were spent in providing services from which rate payers benefited. An alternative is to suppose that the proceeds are used not to increase expenditure but to permit a reduction of other taxes.[1]

But whereas Turvey chose to assume a reduction of income tax to offset the rise in rates, we shall instead assume that one real estate tax system replaces another, leaving revenue, and hence expenditure, unchanged. For this purpose we shall use tax No. 1, an ad valorem tax on the value of site only, as a

[1] *The Economics of Real Property: An Analysis of Property Values and Patterns of Use* (New York, Macmillan, 1957), p. 67.

starting point and examine the consequences of replacing it successively with each of the six other alternatives. Short-run effects will be examined in this chapter, long-run effects in Chapter 8.

Tax No. 1

A site-value tax is a convenient starting point for two reasons, first, because, as will be argued, it is neutral both to operating and investment decisions, second, because it cannot be shifted from owners to tenants.

Tax No. 1 is neutral to operating decisions because, as was pointed out in Chapter 6, site value is independent of the value or condition of the particular improvement that exists on the site. The tax therefore does not vary with operating outlays, and the post-tax optimum operating point is the same as the pre-tax optimum.

The conclusion that a tax on site value cannot be shifted from owner to tenant is almost universally assented to by tax analysts on the ground that site rent is a pure economic surplus. The only necessary caution is that the value of drainage, leveling, or other improvements to the site must not be included in the tax base. Although the question of tax shifting will not be taken up until the next chapter, the matter is mentioned here because it affects the equilibrium from which our comparisons begin. Since tax No. 1 cannot be shifted, it does not affect the height of the revenue-cost curve, gross of tax, even in the long run. Hence, we may draw the initial equilibrium as one in which the revenue-cost curves of all firms are tangent to the 45-degree line, while the net revenue-cost curves are below them by the amount of the tax. This procedure involves assuming that present owners owned the property at the time the site-value tax was first imposed, which is convenient because it allows us to avoid the analytically empty steps of first capitalizing the tax in a reduction of land value and cost and then capitalizing its removal (when other taxes are substituted for tax No. 1) as an exactly equal increase in land value and cost.

Tax No. 2

If the electorate now decides to adopt tax No. 2, the present American real estate tax, in place of tax No. 1, while holding revenue constant, what will be the effect on quality of operation? The answer for the short run must be that there will be none, for tax No. 2, like tax No. 1, is apparently neutral to operating decisions. It was argued in Chapter 6 that assessed value tends to equal market value, which in turn presumes optimum operation of the property, and that therefore the amount of tax paid on a property does not vary with the actual manner in which the owner operates. Graphically, tax No. 2 gives rise to a net revenue-cost curve parallel to the pre-tax curve in the vertical direction. Therefore, the optimum operating point is not displaced by the tax, and, in the short run, tax No. 2 does not affect the quality of operation.

The distribution of the tax burden among owners, however, will not be the same as for tax No. 1, the site-value tax. Unless the ratio of building value to site value is the same for all properties (and we know that it is not), some owners will be paying more tax and some less than before. Those who own properties for which the ratio of building value to site value exceeds the average for the jurisdiction will find their tax bills raised; those for whose property the ratio is less than the average will find their tax bills reduced.[2] The latter receive a windfall gain, the former suffer a loss (at least until part of tax No. 2 can be shifted to the tenants). These gains and losses exactly offset one another in the short run. Thus, if, as is the case in the United States, land and improvements are

[2] Using extensive samples, Robert M. Haig studied the redistribution of the burden that would have occurred in New York City under the 1915 proposal to place the whole real estate levy on a site-value base. As one might have expected, a pattern emerged in which housing far from the center and therefore on less valuable land was almost always found to have its tax load reduced by the change, while housing near the center often had its tax bill raised. One cannot, however, readily translate this into a pattern by rent class, since low-and high-rent buildings were found both near to and far from the center. *Some Probable Effects of the Exemption of Improvements from Taxation in the City of New York*, a report prepared for the Committee on Taxation of the City of New York (New York, 1915), *passim*.

usually owned in common, the real-property-owning class as a whole neither gains nor loses income in the short run as a result of the tax change. Consequently, the income of all other consuming classes, including the tenant class, is also unchanged. Hence, there can be no income effect on housing demand from the tax change and therefore no shift in revenue-cost curves induced by changes in demand.

Tax No. 3

Unlike taxes No. 1 and No. 2, tax No. 3, a gross-rent levy, is not neutral to operating decisions. The net revenue-cost curve resulting from the tax is flatter than the pre-tax curve. Hence, by comparison with tax No. 1 this tax shifts the optimum operating point to the left, toward lower quality of operation. The shift for a given tax rate, however, is not so large as would appear from examination of the revenue-cost curve of a single firm, since as all firms reduce quality simultaneously, each firm finds its rents shrinking less than would be the case for single-firm changes in quality. On the other hand, the condition that tax No. 3 must yield the same revenue as the tax it replaced gives rise to a contrary effect. If the rate of tax on gross rent is set initially to yield the required revenue, then as quality of operation is reduced and gross rent falls, the yield will fall short of the initial goal and the rate will have to be increased. This will further flatten the net revenue-cost curves and yield a final short-run equilibrium at a lower level of quality than would have obtained with the initial gross-rent tax rates.

As between properties, the extent of the effects of the tax change on quality and on net income would not necessarily be uniform but would depend upon the precise relationship between fixed costs, operating costs, and gross rent in each case. For the rental-housing industry as a whole, however, these general conclusions follow: As firms adjust to the tax, they move to the left and down along their revenue-cost curves. When the final short-run equilibrium has been reached, the industry's total tax bill will (by assumption) be the same as before the tax change. But in moving leftward, every firm will have reduced rent *more* than cost (this follows from the shape of the revenue-cost curves); hence, net income for the industry as a whole must be reduced. If consumers spend on other goods the whole amount saved through the reduction of rental outlays, the income of other sectors will rise. An equal proportion of all owners and all nonowners are likely to be included in the tenant class. We conclude that since the fall in owners' incomes is probably offset by a rise in nonowners' incomes, the income of the tenant class is likely to be unchanged, and there will be no income effect on the demand for rental housing.

Tax No. 4

Tax No. 4 is a levy on the net income of real property. Like tax No. 1 and No. 2, it is neutral to operating decisions, since the net revenue-cost curve to which it gives rise is parallel to the 45-degree line at the same level of cost as is the curve gross of tax. The argument is, of course, analogous to the conventional proposition that a tax on net income will not affect the price or quantity of output of a profit-maximizing firm. Like the conventional producer, the rental-housing operator chooses his most profitable level of output before the tax is imposed; it remains the most profitable output even though the government takes x percent of the net return in taxes.[3]

---

[3] Since these propositions are difficult to demonstrate graphically, the following mathematical proof is offered:

Let the functional relationship of rent to cost be expressed as $Rent = R(c)$, where $c = cost$, not including normal profit. Then profit at any level of quality $= R(c) - c$.

Now suppose tax No. 4 to be levied at rate t, where t is positive but less than 1. We can then write, for the net revenue-cost curve,

$$Net\ RC_4 = R(c) - t[R(c) - c]$$
$$= R(c)(1 - t) + tc$$

and Slope of net $RC_4 = R'(c)(1 - t) + t$

Maximum profits are earned where the RC curve has unitary slope. Hence, the pre-tax profit optimum occurs where $R'(c) = 1$.

But at that point the slope of net RC_4 is also unitary, since $(1 - t) + t = 1$.

Moreover, at all points where $0 < R'(c) < 1$ the slope of net $RC_4 < 1$, and at all points where $R'(c) > 1$ the slope of net $RC_4 > 1$.

Hence, the slope of net RC_4 equals unity only at the quality point at which the slope of RC_4 equals unity. Therefore, the post-tax optimum occurs at the same quality level as the pre-tax optimum.

Hence, changing from tax No. 1 to tax No. 4 will not affect quality of operation in the short run. As in the case of other changes, it is likely to cause a redistribution of the tax burden among property owners but will leave their total income unchanged and hence have no income effects on housing demand.

Tax No. 5

Although the British "rates," our tax No. 5, are levied on the tenant rather than the landlord and are therefore not easily handled in our model, we shall attempt to analyze them in terms consistent with our discussion of other taxes. We assume as before that the rental-housing industry is in long-run equilibrium before the changeover from site-value taxation to "rates." This means that landlords have everywhere made the best rent bargains they can with tenants. If "rates" are now imposed upon tenants, tenants will no longer be willing to pay the same rents as before but will wish to reduce rents by the amount of the tax due. We conclude that they will succeed in doing so as leases expire because the landlord's supply curve of space is perfectly inelastic in the short run and because the long-run market equilibrium we start from rules out any sort of housing shortage.[4]

If it be granted that the tax is passed back to the landlord in the short run, then tax No. 5 can be treated as a variant of tax No. 3, the gross-rent tax, the principal difference being, as explained in Chapter 6, that the effective rate of tax No. 5 against gross rent is progressive rather than proportional because, although the "rate" itself is proportional, the allowable percentage deductions are regressive to gross rent. The conclusion that tax No. 3 would cause a reduction in quality of operation holds also for tax No. 5. The only difference is that because tax No. 5 is effectively progressive, it will have a stronger effect than tax No. 3 on high-rent housing and a weaker effect on low.

[4] For a somewhat different conclusion see Ursula K. Hicks, *Public Finance* (London, Cambridge University Press, 1947), pp. 190–98. Mrs. Hicks concludes that tenants will be able to shift a large part of any increase in rates to the landlord in a declining area but at best only a small part in an expanding area.

These conclusions, however, are based on the theory of "rates" rather than on current British practice, for ratable values in housing have long been held at the level that obtained on June 30, 1939. In effect, then, the tax is currently a fixed one with respect to operating outlays and has the same effect as tax No. 1.[5]

Tax No. 6

Tax No. 6 is a tax abatement designed to encourage a higher level of quality of operation. As described in Chapter 6 and illustrated in Figure 6.4, the abatement would consist of an agreement between the taxing authority and the landlord not to raise the assessment (or other tax base) during some specified term if the landlord undertakes certain desirable improvements. Such an agreement would convert the owner's tax liability, at whatever amount it then stood, into a constant liability (given the tax rate) for all levels of quality higher than the one at which he was then operating.

So far as operating improvements are concerned, such an abatement has little claim to our attention. It would be useful only in the case of tax No. 3, the gross-rent levy, or tax No. 5, the British "rates," the initial effect of which is to reduce quality of operation. In these cases the abatement would exactly offset the initial unfavorable impact effect—owners would be led back to the same level of quality at which they would have operated in the absence of any tax. This is so because the constant liability resulting from the abatement leaves the owner with a net RC_0 curve that is parallel to his original RC curve in the range of quality above the point at which the abatement becomes effective. The abatement thus converts tax No. 3 or No. 5 into the equivalent of tax No. 1.

The tax No. 6 abatement involves no direct loss of tax revenue, since the properties receiving the benefit continue to pay the same amounts as before. There may be indirect losses, however, if the rise in rents of refurbished units is achieved at the expense of gross rents of other properties and thereby

[5] See note 5 of Chapter 6 in this book.

diminishes the tax base of such properties. Following this chain of reasoning to its remote end, we discover that if we wished to maintain tax revenue at its initial level, we *might* have to raise the tax rate, which, of course, would tend to offset the initial favorable effect of the abatement on those properties subject to it by further depressing quality of operation in those buildings not so benefited.

Tax No. 6 is more likely to be useful for its long-run investment effects than for its effects on short-run operating decisions.

Tax No. 7

Tax No. 7 is a tax penalty applied to all properties that fall below some specified minimum standard quality. An example of such a penalty is illustrated in Figure 6.5. The purpose of such a penalty would not be to influence quality of operation by altering the slope of the net RC curve but to influence it by introducing a gross discontinuity at the minimum standard level, such that no operating point to the left of the standard would be as profitable as operation at the standard point itself. (The penalty would never raise an owner higher than the minimum standard.) Hence, the penalty approach can only be successful if the sub-optimum it creates below the standard quality level is clearly less profitable than operation at the standard itself. Unfortunately, this condition will not always be fulfilled. If the penalty illustrated in Figure 6.5 is made sufficiently small, it is apparent that the optimum along net RC_7 below the standard quality level could turn out to be more profitable than operation at the standard itself. Moreover, the farther to the right one sets the standard, the more likely any given penalty is to produce a ruling optimum at less than the standard level. (This point can be verified by extending the net revenue curve in Figure 6.5 out to the right-hand margin and then moving the vertical standard line step by step to the right.) Therefore, the higher the standard, the higher must be the penalty to insure the desired effect.

If the penalty is a fixed sum for each building, then in those unfortunate cases where the below-standard optimum continues to rule, that level of quality will at least be no lower than the level at which the building was operated before imposition of the penalty, for the penalty will not change the slope of the pre-penalty net RC curve. This is the case illustrated in Figure 6.5, where the penalty consists of a percentage increase in tax No. 2, the traditional American levy. But if a percentage penalty is applied in connection with tax No. 3 or No. 5, the gross-rent tax and the British "rates," respectively, then it further flattens the net RC curve and insures that the below-standard optimum will be at an even lower quality than the pre-penalty optimum. We have pointed out that the higher the standard, the higher must be the penalty to make it effective. Now we discover that for some tax-plus-penalty combinations, the higher the standard and the higher the penalty, the more harmful the result on those buildings for which the penalty does not make the standard effective. Finally, and more important, it is possible that high penalties combined with high standards will simply cause some owners of very low-quality buildings to withdraw them from the housing supply. Indeed, that may be one of the (perhaps irrational) aims of a tax-penalty policy.

In any event, tax penalties are almost certain to increase tax revenues if they are used in connection with taxes like No. 3 and No. 5 that increase with quality. If the penalties are fully effective, so that every building rises to the minimum standard level, no one will be paying penalties, but payments of the basic tax will rise with quality. Those buildings that were above the minimum standard before the penalty might suffer lower rents through competition with the improved buildings, and the tax base for such properties might shrink, but this effect would not fully offset the growth in the tax base of the buildings that improved. If the penalty is not fully effective, then those buildings that have not improved are at least paying penalties. Only if the perverse effect of penalties in reducing quality were so strong that those buildings that fell to a lower quality level ended by paying less in taxes and penalties combined than they formerly paid in taxes alone could total tax revenues drop.

If the basic tax to which a penalty is added is constant for each building, like tax No. 1 on site value or No. 2 on site and improvement value combined, then there will be no change in revenue if the penalty is fully effective. To the extent that it is not fully effective, tax revenues will rise by the amount of the collected penalties. This rise would then permit the basic tax rate to be lowered, which would have favorable effects on investment decisions but none on operating decisions, since a constant tax is neutral with respect to the latter.

Summary

In Table 7.1 we summarize our conclusions concerning the short-run effects of real estate taxes on quality of operation. The effects are those that we would expect to observe after owners have had time to adjust their quality of operation to the tax but before there has been any opportunity to recover normal profits by raising rents per unit. The fact that the latter adjustment may begin before the former is completed does not prevent us from separating them conceptually.

The effects in question apply to all qualities of rental housing for taxes No. 1 through No. 5. Taxes No. 6 and No. 7, however, would probably affect only low-quality units.

TABLE 7.1

Operating Effects of Alternative Taxes[a]

Tax Type	Effect on Quality of Operation
No. 2 (assessed value of land and improvements)	Neutral
No. 3 (gross rent)	Negative
No. 4 (net income)	Neutral
No. 5 (British "rates")	Negative
No. 6 (abatement)	Neutral
No. 7 (penalty)	Uncertain: negative to positive

[a] Short-run effects on quality of operation compared with effect of tax No. 1 as a neutral standard.

CHAPTER EIGHT

THE
EFFECT OF LOCAL
REAL ESTATE TAXES
ON INVESTMENT
DECISIONS

In the short run, changes in the real estate tax system affect operating outlays of existing rental-housing firms. In the longer run, effects on investment decisions will be observed. If the industry was in full equilibrium before the tax change, then the change will usually disturb that equilibrium, and a new one will be reached only after investment has been shaped by the new tax system over a period of many years. At the new equilibrium, the standing stock of housing is likely to be of a different size and character from the stock at the beginning. The task of this chapter will be to deduce the probable nature of those changes.

Although we are now primarily concerned with investment effects, we must continue to deal with operating effects as well, in order to discover whether the long-run process of tax shifting can be expected to alter operating outlays in existing buildings. A changeover from tax No. 1, the site-value levy, to any of the taxes that bear on building rent (i.e., to any other of the seven types) would profoundly disturb the equilibrium of the rental-housing industry. We shall examine in detail the long-run adjustments that would occur in the case of a change to tax No. 2, the traditional American levy and, as we proceed, describe any differences that appear probable for the other cases.

Regardless of how the change from tax No. 1 to tax No. 2 rearranged the distribution of the tax load among existing housing properties, tax No. 2 would immediately fall as a new burden upon all projects for investing in structure. Anyone contemplating new construction, remodeling, or the replacement of structural parts and equipment would now have to pay a tax on the values so created, where formerly none was paid, and in the analysis that follows investment effects will be considered under those three headings.

If, as we assume, new capital invested in rental housing was previously able to earn the same return as capital invested at the margin elsewhere, then the changeover to tax No. 2 would push housing investment below the prevailing margin and cut it off entirely until such time as housing profits rose sufficiently so that after real estate taxes they were once again equal at the margin to the rate of return elsewhere. We assume throughout that due allowance is made for differences in risk as between various kinds of investment, and we leave out of account the fact that a tax on housing capital may reduce the equilibrium rate of return to capital in general.[1]

Recalling the discussion of land rent in Chapter 3, we see that the above statement stands without modification on the "classical assumption" that if a tax is levied on the combined rent of land and improvements, its burden will be divided between the two bases in the proportion that land rent bears to building rent (Simon's case No. 4). The changeover from tax No. 1 to tax No. 2 relieves land of a part of the tax; and on the classical assumption the full amount of such relief would eventually be capitalized as an increase in the value of land,

[1] On this point, see Herbert A. Simon, "The Incidence of a Tax on Urban Real Property," in Richard A. Musgrave and Carl S. Shoup, eds., *Readings in the Economics of Taxation* (Homewood, Ill., Richard D. Irwin, 1959), pp. 416–35, and the works by Harry Gunnison Brown cited therein.

so that the cost of using land (annual capital cost plus annual taxes) would remain exactly the same as before. Thus, reduction in the land tax would not reduce costs for prospective investors, while a tax on buildings would raise them by the full amount of the tax.

A different answer is obtained, however, if we examine the question under our second hypothesis, which holds that when a tax is levied on the combined value of land and improvements, the landowner will bear *more* than that proportion of the tax attributable to land value. In that case, shifting from a site-value tax to a combined-value tax would reduce the value or rent of land gross of tax, and the reduction in land rent would stand as a partial offset to the increase in building costs. Under extreme assumptions, such an offset might be equal to or greater than the rise in building costs, but no student of the subject has thought this to be at all likely. We shall therefore confine ourselves to considering the possibility of a partial offset (Simon's case No. 3).

With or without the partial offset, the building tax inhibits further investment in housing until profits are restored to normal. This in turn will happen when that portion of the tax upon buildings which has not been shifted backward to landowners has been shifted forward to tenants. Such a shift occurs when the rent of buildings has risen by an amount equal to the remaining burden of the tax, either as a result of a decrease in the stock of housing or of an upward shift in the demand for it.

A decrease in the stock will take place if, on account of the building tax, new housing is not built so fast as old housing is razed or converted to other uses. Assuming tastes constant, an increase in demand will take place if either population or income rises, as described in Chapter 3. With no change on the demand side, a decrease in supply—that is, in the standing stock of housing—will effectively increase rents. If population or income is decreasing, however, the standing stock might have to shrink for many years before the tax could be passed on to tenants.

Effect of Tax Change on Rate of Replacement of Structure

Before we examine the shifting process, it is necessary to analyze the impact effect of the tax change on the investment decisions of owners of the standing stock. The decisions in question are those dealing with rate of replacement of worn structure and equipment, or with what we have called "condition of structure."

We have argued that the structural condition of a building can be summarized in the value of the term $1/L$, the average period of replacement of structure actually adhered to by the owner. As explained in Chapter 2, in equilibrium owners will have carried replacement of structure to the point where an additional dollar per year spent on it is expected to yield just one additional dollar of rent.

In this setting, a change from tax No. 1 (on site value) to tax No. 2 (on combined value of site and improvement) will not directly affect the rate of replacement. Each owner will find his optimum rate of replacement unaffected by the tax change. The pre-tax optimum was at that level where the marginal outlay to increase the rate of replacement just equaled the marginal rent return which it was expected to produce (and the marginal returns per dollar of outlay were diminishing). Tax No. 2 is based on market value, which, in turn, represents the present value of expected future net income. Expected future net income will vary with changes in the rate of replacement, but the tax will take the same proportion of expected net income at any level of replacement outlay. Hence, expected net income after tax will be maximized at the same level of replacement outlay as expected net income before tax, and the tax will not affect the owner's rate of replacement of structure.

Graphically, a fall in the rate of replacement is shown by a contraction of the distance FC, which extends from the origin to the point of intersection of the revenue-cost curve and the cost axis. When the rate of replacement is reduced, it can be assumed that tenants will pay less rent than formerly, even

though operating services are not changed. We need not assume, however, that operating services are held constant. In any
case, as the revenue-cost curve shifts to the left, it also loses
some of its elevation.

In Figure 8.1 *RC* was tangent to the 45-degree line at point

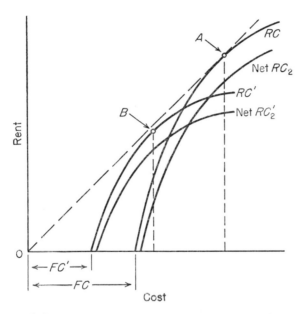

FIGURE 8.1   A CHANGE IN THE RATE OF REPLACEMENT

A, before the tax change. Upon impact, tax No. 2 left the
owner with after-tax revenues indicated by net *RC*₂. Suppose
that by reducing the rate of replacement, the owner then moved
the curve to the left, arriving finally at the relationship shown
by *RC'*. The optimum operating point, *B*, on *RC'* must lie below the 45-degree line, for the marginal loss of rent exceeds the
marginal reduction in replacement outlay below the initial
optimum. The loss of income before taxes on account of the
shift from *A* to *B* is shown by the vertical distance from *B* to
the diagonal. But, as argued above, under tax No. 2, the
reduction in taxes attendant upon moving from *A* to *B* will be

only a fraction of the reduction in income and so will not fully offset it. Therefore, the move cannot pay.

A similar argument applies if the change is from tax No. 1 to tax No. 4 (a net-income tax) instead of to tax No. 2: the optimum rate of replacement will not be affected.

On the other hand, a change to either tax No. 3 (a gross-rent tax) or tax No. 5 (the British "rates") would cause a reduction in replacement outlays. Suppose a tax to be levied at rate t on gross rent (or at the equivalent rate on ratable value in the case of tax No. 5). Either of these taxes reduces marginal rent receipts per dollar of marginal outlay on replacement. After the tax change, the optimum level of replacement occurs at the point where the marginal outlay for that purpose equals the marginal rent return multiplied by $(1 - t)$. As a consequence of diminishing marginal returns of rent per dollar of marginal outlay on replacement, this point will be at a lower level of replacement than the optimum before the tax change.

The effects of taxes No. 6 and No. 7 on rate of replacement of structure will be taken up later in this chapter.

Up to this point we have been discussing the direct, or impact, effects of tax changes on rate of replacement. These are the effects that would occur before any tax shifting takes place. We are now ready to analyze the effects of tax shifting, under three different assumptions: (1) population and income constant, supply diminishes; (2) population constant, supply diminishes, income rises; and (3) income constant, supply diminishes, population rises.

Tax No. 2 Shifted by Reduction of Supply

Consider now the case in which tax No. 2, the traditional American levy, is substituted for tax No. 1, the site-value tax, none of the building portion of the tax is shifted back onto landowners, housing demand remains stable, and the portion of the tax levied on buildings is shifted to tenants through a shrinkage of supply. We have now established that the tax change will not directly affect the rate of replacement of structure, i.e., the condition of the structure, in existing buildings. Since the condition of structure is unchanged, revenue-cost curves remain as before, and, as was shown in Chapter 7, the tax change does not affect the optimum level of operating outlay along given revenue-cost curves.

The only significant immediate result of the tax change is the redistribution of the tax burden among property owners. New construction will not halt until the price of land begins to rise in response to the tax relief to land. Once this price rise is under way, however, construction will be pushed below the margin of profitability, and new building will cease because (as explained above) the new tax on building is just offset by the relief to land, leaving new construction costs constant if land prices remain constant but higher if land prices rise. According to the classical assumption, land prices will eventually rise by the whole capitalized value of the tax relief; therefore, new construction costs will rise as well.

Once new construction halts, the stage is set for shifting forward to tenants the portion of tax No. 2 which falls on buildings. The shift will take place as housing structures are razed by fire or disaster (including war) or are replaced by other uses and the eliminated units are not matched by new construction because of the tax disincentive. Consequently, the standing stock of housing will diminish, and since population and income remain constant, rents will rise. Since the price elasticity of demand for space is low (see Chapter 3), a relatively small diminution of the standing stock will cause a relatively large rise in rent.

In the simplified model we deal with here, it is impossible to specify the rent levels at which the stock will diminish most. It seems likely, however, that old housing involving the greatest degree of design obsolescence would go first, since the investment necessary to remodel it would be inhibited by the tax change.

In whatever brackets the supply of housing diminishes, rents will at once begin to rise, since we assume no vacancies to start with. Displaced families will be accommodated because, as rents rise, other tenants will be forced to rent less space, double up, or take in roomers. The rise in rents will take the form of an upward shift of the revenue-cost curves, accompanied by some tendency to flatten out. These motions must be separately explained. One consists of an upward parallel shift, indicating a rise in the price of space as tenants compete for quarters. A second is a reduction in the slopes of the curves as the demand for quality diminishes on account of adverse income effects. The demand for quality depends importantly upon income. The changeover to tax No. 2 leaves total income constant but somewhat alters its after-tax distribution. Once the portion of the tax falling on buildings has been shifted to tenants, the redistribution consists of a gain for landowners at the expense of tenants, whose real income falls on account of the rise in rents. Some, but not all, landowners will be tenants, so the net effect will be a decline in the real income of tenants.

Since the income elasticity of demand for quality is high and rent is a substantial element in family budgets, this income effect may be strong enough to reduce appreciably the demand for quality, and a reduction in the demand for quality results in tenants on the average being willing to pay less than they previously did for the elements of service provided by the owner's operating outlays. For a given condition of structure, this means a flatter revenue-cost curve. This tendency to flatten out will be partially offset by a substitution effect in favor of quality as the price of space rises. We assume, however, that the income effect outweighs the substitution effect, so that the outcome is a reduction in the slopes of revenue-cost curves.

Over the longer run, as was argued above, the condition of structure also becomes variable, so that there is a third element to the adjustment of demand as the tax is shifted. The condition of existing structures is an element in housing quality. Hence, if there is an adverse effect on demand for quality because of tax shifting, the demand for good condition of structure will diminish. This change in demand will have the effect of reducing for each owner the marginal rent return obtainable from marginal outlays on replacement and will encourage a general reduction in structural replacement.

The net result of the three motions combined is that (1) buildings will be maintained at a lower quality of structure than before; (2) the revenue-cost curves for these lower qualities of structure will be higher but also flatter than they would have been before the tax shift; and (3) because the curves are flatter, the optimum quality of operation will be lower than it would have been in structures of similar quality before the tax shift.

More generally, we may say that the shifting process increases space rent, since the supply of space is inelastic while new construction is in abeyance. This rise in space rent has adverse income effects on the demand for quality, which are only partially offset by favorable substitution effects, and since the supply of quality is elastic, less quality is supplied.

Space rents will continue to increase until the prospective return on housing is high enough to discourage all further razing or to make new construction possible once again. This suggests a further distinction to be analyzed. We may conceive of two different cost situations for the construction industry. In one case costs are such that private new construction is economically feasible at the equilibrium rent levels, before the tax change, in all rent brackets. In the other case, more like the prevailing situation in the United States, private new construction is no longer feasible for the lower end of the rent distribution even before the tax change, because the cost of construction inputs has risen so much in the past and/or because housing and building codes have made very cheap construction illegal.

In the first case, the flow of new construction suffices to keep rents stable in all rent brackets before the tax change. After the change, space rents rise in all brackets until new construction is once more profitable and then stabilize with new construction just sufficient to replace any buildings razed after that time in each bracket plus or minus the net change due to "moving" of buildings. (For the market as a whole, of course, plus and minus changes due to moving cancel out.) In the second case, the same sequence appears in the upper rent brackets, where new construction was profitable before the change. In the lower rent brackets before the tax change, two further variants are likely. Either space rents were increasing gradually as the net effect of moving and razing reduced the standing stock, or else they were stable at a level at which the net gain from moving offset the loss through disaster, demolition, and conversion to other uses.

In the first variant, rents would continue to rise but at an increasing pace, for the cessation of new construction, by causing rents in the upper brackets to rise, would tend to reduce or cut off the flow of buildings moving down to the lower brackets. In the second variant, likewise, moving down would either be slowed or stopped, and this would cause the previously stable lower rents to begin to increase. Thus, whether new construction takes place only at the top or at all levels makes no great difference in this context. Either way, the effect of the tax change is to raise rents at all levels of the rent distribution as the tax-shifting process takes place.

Finally, it should be noted that when new construction resumes, the average structural quality and quality of operating service in the new buildings will be lower than before the tax change, for the same income effects which operated to reduce the demand for quality in the standing stock would also affect the demand for quality in new units.

So far we have assumed that none of the building tax is passed back to landowners in the form of reduced site rent, an assumption which is perhaps less plausible when the building tax is shifted by a decline in the standing stock with housing demand constant than when it is shifted at least in part by a rise in housing demand. If we assume instead that a portion of the building tax is offset by reduced site rent, how will the above conclusions as to the quality effects of the change from tax No. 1 to tax No. 2 be altered? The answer is that the magnitude of all the effects will be reduced because there will be less tax to pass on, hence a smaller rise in revenue-cost curves, a smaller income and substitution effect, and a less substantial decline in demand for quality.

Tax No. 2 Shifted by Rising Income

Next consider the case in which tax No. 2, on the combined value of land and building, is substituted for tax No. 1, the site-value tax, none of the building part of the tax is shifted back onto landowners, and population (i.e., number of households) is constant, but real income per household is increasing in all income classes. We shall restrict the analysis to the case in which new private construction is feasible only in the higher rent brackets, on the understanding that the results would be broadly the same in the case where new construction is feasible at all rent levels.

When, in the first case examined, we assumed housing demand to be constant, we were able to describe a market that was essentially static before the tax change. With income rising, however, the market will not have been static before the changeover, and we must now describe the pattern of market development that will have been taking place in order to compare it with the situation after tax No. 2 is introduced.

Since the income elasticity of demand for housing quality is high, a rise in real income will lead to a pronounced rise in demand for quality. The income elasticity of demand for space is apparently much lower but still positive, so that rising income will lead to a less pronounced increase in the demand for space.[2] With tax No. 1, the site-value levy, in force, suppliers are in no way inhibited from adapting to the evolving pattern of demand by new construction, remodeling, changes in the rate of replacement of structure, and changes in operating outlays. Broadly speaking, the result will be a gradual increase

[2] When income rises, some family units that were living doubled up seek separate quarters, so that the number of separately residing households can increase even when population is constant.

in the standing stock of housing and a gradual increase in the average quality both of structure and operation.

The change will come about through the combination of tenants moving upward through the quality distribution of housing and of the stock itself adapting to the new income distribution of tenants. As tenants move up the income-rent-quality ladder, the demand for space in the upper ranges will increase, both as a result of tenants moving up from lower brackets and because those already in the upper brackets will want more space as their income rises. In the lower brackets, the tendency of tenants to move out might conceivably be offset by the rising demand for space on the part of those who remain behind. All one can say positively is that demand for space will not rise so much, relatively, as in the higher brackets and is likely to fall, especially in the worst grades of housing. Owners of the latter therefore may find net income falling and may decide to remodel, raze, or board up their properties.

At the upper end of the scale, where new construction is possible, it will take place whenever the pressure of rising demand gives the signal. In those brackets, new construction will thus tend to prevent any rise in the revenue-cost curves of existing housing, but there will be many rent levels at which the new income distribution faced by the old rent distribution of housing makes manifest a shortage of space, and some of these rent levels are likely to be below the building margin. In such brackets, a housing shortage will appear and rents will begin to rise. To the extent that the number of families wishing to live in such houses is greater than before, revenue-cost curves will rise mainly in the parallel sense, indicating a rise in space rents. To the extent that the families living in such houses have higher average incomes than before (and they may not have, since families will be moving out at the upper end of the bracket as well as in at the lower), the demand for quality as well as for space will be increasing. The outcome, however, is complicated by the fact that the rising price of space will have a substitution effect favorable to demand for quality and an income effect adverse to it. Thus, we cannot specify what the net effect on demand for quality will be in such brackets.

In the brackets where revenue-cost curves rise, assuming that they do not rise enough to make new construction feasible, the increased return to building owners will encourage an inward movement of buildings from brackets where demand is less strong. For example, it might become profitable to remodel buildings that were losing tenants at the low end of the rent scale in order to move them up into a different bracket. In any case, such adaptation of the stock to the changing pattern of demand is at a maximum under tax No. 1, a site-value tax, which has no disincentive effects upon investment.

If now tax No. 1 is replaced by tax No. 2 on combined value of site and improvement, how does this picture change? Tax No. 2 will cut off new construction and remodeling by pressing the return to these investments below the margin of profitability. With new construction cut off, tenants will be unable to move up the ladder into better housing. Rising income will, however, have two effects: the demand for more space as income rises will cause revenue-cost curves to rise in the parallel sense, and the demand for more quality will cause them to become steeper. The rise in the price of space as income rises will have substitution effects slightly favorable to the demand for quality and income effects adverse to it, the combined effect of which will be partly to offset the rise in the demand for quality. The net result, however, will be some rise in the demand for quality and hence in the quality of operation and rate of replacement of structure.

With new construction in abeyance, the standing stock will not be stable but will begin to diminish as a consequence of razing, disaster, and so on. This decrease will further aggravate the shortage of space and cause a further rise in rent per room and a further reduction in the real income of tenants. This chain of events, combined with the rise in space rent from rising demand, could conceivably have a sufficiently strong adverse income effect to reduce the demand for quality even while money income is rising.

Just when, in this process of complex adjustment, one can speak of tax No. 2 having been at last "shifted to tenants" is not clear. Probably the moment at which rents have risen high enough to encourage a sustained resumption of new construction is as good as any. At that moment, how will things stand by comparison, not with the situation before the tax change but with the situation that would then obtain had the tax change not occurred?

1. The size of the standing stock will be smaller than it would have been, and rents on the average will be higher. Crowding of tenants will have increased.

2. The average quality of the buildings in the standing stock will be lower than it would have been, since new construction, consisting of above-average-quality units, will have been in abeyance.

3. Adaptation of the standing stock to changes in demand will have been inhibited by the tax disincentive to remodeling.

4. Whether quality of operation and quality of structure in the existing buildings will be higher or lower than would have been the case in the same buildings without tax No. 2 is not clear, since tenants' money income will be higher but their real income may be either higher or lower than before the tax change. That is not the meaningful comparison, however, since the standing stock would have consisted of different buildings but for the tax. More meaningful is the fact that tenants real income will be lower than it would have been had the tax change not been made, and the demand for quality will consequently be lower. Since the supply of quality via operating and replacement outlays is elastic, it may reasonably be concluded that fewer of these elements of quality will be supplied to the market as a whole than would have been the case if the tax change had not been made.

To the extent that a fraction of the tax on improvements is shifted back onto landowners in the form of reduced site rent gross of tax instead of forward onto tenants in the form of higher building rent, all of the above effects will be reduced in magnitude.

Tax No. 2 Shifted by Rising Population

We may now, more briefly, review the case in which tax No. 2, on the combined value of site and improvement, is shifted by the growth in population, with the average level of income and its distribution by size unchanged. We start with the fact that demand for space will be increasing at all levels of quality. If, before the tax change, new construction is possible only at the upper rent levels, the demand for more space at low rents would have to be met entirely by moving old buildings down. When tax No. 2 is introduced, new construction halts, and a housing shortage develops at all rent levels, since population is increasing uniformly throughout the income distribution, and razing gradually reduces the standing stock. Rent charged per room will begin to rise where it has been stable or to rise faster where it has risen before. With money income constant, tenants' real income will now begin to fall. This will have an adverse effect on their demand for quality, offset only in part by the substitution effect in the opposite direction.

When the process of tax shifting is completed and new construction resumes, the situation will be as follows:

1. The size of the standing stock will be smaller than it would have been, and rents will be higher at all levels of the rent distribution. Crowding of tenants will have increased.

2. Tenants' real incomes will be lower at all levels of the income distribution. This reduces the demand for quality (despite the substitution effect in the opposite direction) and has a number of consequences: (*a*) new construction, when it resumes, will be of a lower average quality than it was before; (*b*) revenue-cost curves, although at a higher level, are less steep than they would have been, and consequently buildings are operated at a lower level of quality; and (*c*) similarly, the average period of replacement of structure increases (i.e., condition of structure is worse).

3. Adaptation of the standing stock to changes in the pattern of demand occasioned by changes in real income, or in taste or technology, will have been inhibited by the tax disincentive to remodeling.

Once again, these effects will be greater if all of the tax on improvements is shifted forward onto tenants; they will be less to the extent that a portion of the tax on improvements is shifted back onto landowners in the form of reduced site-rent gross of tax.

The Effects of Other Taxes Compared with Those of Tax No. 2

Broadly speaking the deleterious effects on quality of a change from tax No. 1 to tax No. 2 come about, regardless of assumptions as to income or population trends, in two ways: first, through the disincentive effect on new construction and remodeling which inhibits adaptation of the standing stock to the pattern of demand; second, through adverse income effects resulting from the rise in rent. Tax No. 2, it should be noted, does not have direct effects on either operating decisions or decisions as to the optimum rate of replacement of structure.

However, a change from tax No. 1 to either tax No. 3, on gross rent, or tax No. 5, the British "rates," beside having all the effects recited above, would also directly reduce quality of operation and condition of structure by changing the optimum level of operating outlay and the optimum rate of replacement. Thus, either of these taxes would be more harmful to housing quality than tax No. 2.

On the oher hand, the results of changing from tax No. 1 to tax No. 4, on real estate net income, would be about the same as those for changing to tax No. 2. The choice between tax No. 2 and tax No. 4 must be made on grounds other than effects on quality.

The Effects of Tax No. 6

Tax No. 6, a tax abatement for the purpose of encouraging desirable improvements in existing buildings, must, of course, be used in combination with one of the five basic taxes. Since the abatement under examination takes the form of an agreement not to raise the tax base if certain improvements are undertaken rather than an agreement to lower the tax base, its combination with tax No. 1 would be meaningless, because the base of tax No. 1 is in any case invariant to changes in the state of improvements on the site. An abatement might, however, be combined with any of the other basic types. In each case we have to consider its long-run, or investment, effects under two headings: (1) effects on the rate of replacement of structure and (2) effects on remodeling. But instead of supposing a change from tax No. 1 to each of the other types combined with tax No. 6, as heretofore, it will suffice to compare the results under each basic tax in combination with the abatement with the results under each basic tax alone, rates being so adjusted as to maintain revenue.

In combination with tax No. 2, the traditional American levy, an abatement would have no effect on the rate of replacement of structure. Under tax No. 2 the tax base for a given structure is already at its maximum because the owner is not induced by the tax to depart from the pre-tax optimum rate of replacement. An agreement not to increase the tax base if the owner increases his rate of replacement therefore will not induce him to do so. On the other hand, an abatement would directly encourage remodeling by removing the tax on any increase in value so created. If the abatement reduces revenue below what it would otherwise have been, the rate of tax will have to be increased. Since tax No. 2 does not affect operating outlays or rates of replacement, the higher rates would not be harmful in those directions, but they would slightly increase the disincentive to new construction. The net effect would be a strong inducement to adapt the standing stock to market conditions through remodeling slightly offset by an increased disincentive to adapt by means of new construction.

In combination with either tax No. 3, on gross rent, or tax No. 5, the British "rates," an abatement would encourage an increased rate of replacement of structure. These taxes, by themselves, induce owners to replace structure at less than the pre-tax optimum rate. The abatement would exactly cancel the harmful effect of either tax by removing its marginal impact. On remodeling, the abatement would have the same favorable effect as in connection with tax No. 2 above, accompanied by the same unfavorable impact on new building.

In combination with tax No. 4, a net-income tax, an abatement would have results similar to those for tax No. 2: it would not affect rate of replacement but would stimulate remodeling partly at the expense of new construction.

The Effects of Tax No. 7

Tax No. 7, a tax penalty to encourage desirable improvements, must, like tax No. 6, be used in combination with one of the five basic taxes. Since state law generally requires equal tax rates for all properties of a given class, we have concluded that penalties would not be feasible except where they could be imposed by way of differential assessments. This would rule out the use of penalties in combination with tax No. 3 or No. 4, since the bases of these taxes are actual gross rent and actual net income rather than assessed quantities. A combination with tax No. 1 can be ruled out on the ground that a tax penalty is unlikely to be used against substandard structures when all other buildings are entirely free of tax. Thus, we need consider penalties only in connection with tax No. 2, on assessed value, or tax No. 5 (the British "rates"), on assessed gross rent less allowable percentage deductions.

Suppose that tax No. 7 is used in combination with tax No. 2 by increasing the assessed valuation of buildings that do not come up to a socially defined minimum standard. The results were examined with regard to a standard of operating service in Chapter 7. If we now extend the idea of a social standard to include structural elements and structural quality, we can examine the effects of tax No. 7 on investment decisions. Consider first its effect on rate of replacement of structure. Suppose that the tax penalty is applied in all buildings where essential equipment performs at less than some specified standard and that to avoid the penalty it is necessary to increase the rate of replacement of structure. Before penalties were imposed, the owner was operating at the point where the marginal outlay on replacement just yielded an equal marginal rent return (for tax No. 2 does not directly affect rate of replacement). Upon imposition of the penalty the owner will either (1) increase the rate of replacement sufficiently to avoid the penalty, (2) continue at the same rate of replacement and pay the penalty, (3) remodel the property to avoid the penalty, (4) raze the structure and put the land to another use, thus avoiding the penalty, (5) board up the property to minimize losses, or (6) abandon the property to avoid all taxes. The owner will choose the most profitable of these alternatives. Which that will be depends upon factors too numerous to spell out.

The situation is not much different if the penalty can be avoided only by remodeling or by installing equipment not previously present (e.g., central heating). Again the owner has a choice of responses. He may remodel, he may do nothing, he may raze, board up, or abandon. The point to note here is that the penalty combined with tax No. 2 is by no means certain to cause owners to improve their properties either by more rapid replacement or by remodeling. Since the direct effects of a penalty are so uncertain, it is impossible to determine the likely effects on revenue and hence on tax rates.

The consequences of combining a penalty with a tax on assessed gross rent, such as tax No. 5, are no more certain than those spelled out above. However, one difference appears. Assume that the penalty consists of a percentage increase in the assessed gross rent of all properties that fail to come up to the standard and that assessed gross rent continues to be set at some ratio to actual gross rent, the ratio being constant for each structure. Then the penalty would raise the effective rate of tax at all levels of quality of a given structure. Earlier in this chapter it was argued that a gross-rent tax will cause owners to move to a lower rate of replacement of structure than would have prevailed under tax No. 1. If the rate of tax is increased, they are induced to move to a still lower rate of replacement.

Thus, the owner upon whom tax No. 7 in combination with tax No. 5 is imposed would have the same options as outlined for the combination with tax No. 2, except that instead of the option of continuing at the same rate of replacement, he would have the option of moving to a still lower one.

Summary

Table 8.1 summarizes the conclusions of this chapter.

TABLE 8.1

Investment Effects of Alternative Taxes [a]

Tax Type	Effect on Rate of Replacement of Structure	Effect on Investment in Remodeling	Effect on Investment in New Construction
No. 2 (assessed value of land and improvement)	Neutral	Negative	Negative
No. 3 (gross rent)	Negative	Negative	Negative
No. 4 (net income)	Neutral	Negative	Negative
No. 5 (British "rates")	Negative	Negative	Negative
No. 6 (abatement)	Neutral	Neutral	Does not apply to new construction
No. 7 (penalty)	Uncertain (may vary from negative to positive)		Does not apply to new construction

[a] Impact effects on rate of replacement, remodeling, and new construction compared with effects of tax No. 1 as a neutral standard.

CHAPTER NINE

A DIGRESSION CONCERNING EVIDENCE

In previous chapters we developed a theory of rental-housing operation and of the structure of the rental-housing market. The theory enabled us to make a number of statements regarding the probable effects of alternative real estate taxes on the maintenance and rehabilitation of urban rental housing. We must now enquire whether the available evidence provides us with any means of testing either the housing theory or the theory of tax incidence based on it.

Evidence Concerning the Operation of Rental Housing

Consider the housing theory first. Its foundation is the proposition that an owner's object is to maximize the net income from an existing rental property by selecting the optimum level of quality of operation and the optimum rate of replacement of structure. We have hypothesized a short run revenue-cost function of a specific kind along which the owner finds his most profitable quality of operation. The relationship between rent receipts and the rate of replacement of structure has also been described as a regular one. What evidence is there that these relationships take the forms described and become the basis for the indicated business decisions?

The only evidence that we have found is in the literature on property management. Property management in the United States has become a profession. Its practitioners are in the business of managing income-producing properties in return

for fees paid to them by owners. Like other professionals, they
have found it useful to circulate their accumulated wisdom:
a *Journal of Property Management* is published quarterly, and
a great many books have been written on the management of
real estate.

Reading through this literature, one discovers a number of
things about the economic basis for property-management decisions. First of all, property managers agree on the point that
their objective is to produce the largest possible net income for
the owner over the economic life of the property. The qualification concerning economic life is introduced because it would
usually be possible to maximize short-run net income by paring
maintenance and operating outlays to the bone, but this is not
conceived to be the objective, since such immediate reductions
in cost impair future net earnings. Rather, the manager takes
into account the whole life-span of the property.

The following quotations are representative of professional
opinion: James C. Downs writes, "Property managers . . . are
judged on their ability to produce the highest possible net
return over a period of years." [1] To quote Atkinson and Frailey,
"The real estate manager goes about his job of producing the
highest possible net income from any given property. He tries
to increase the spread between dollars received in rent and
dollars spent in operation." [2] Or, in the words of William S.
Everett, "Normally, the production of the maximum income
over the economic life of the property is the objective of most
owners." [3]

---

[1] *Principles of Real Estate Management* (Chicago, Institute of Real Estate
Management, 1950), p. 59. Downs also points out that property managers "are
almost universally paid for their services in proportion to their success in the
actual production of gross revenue" (p. 59). It might be suggested that the production of gross rather than of net revenue is therefore likely to become their
actual operating goal, but we prefer to assume that, like other professionals,
property managers are able to put their clients' interests ahead of their own,
in case the two conflict.

[2] H. G. Atkinson and L. E. Frailey, *Fundamentals of Real Estate Practice*
(Englewood Cliffs, N.J., Prentice-Hall, 1946), p. 197.

[3] "Behind That Crystal Ball," *Journal of Property Management*, September,
1960, p. 12.

So much for the economic objective. What about the existence of functional relationships between operating costs and replacement costs on the one hand and gross-rent receipts on the other? Here again the literature comes to the support of our theory. One finds a number of statements indicating that management can choose among various levels of quality of operation and condition of structure and that there exists a discoverable optimum level which it is the object of the manager to attain.

As Everett puts it,

Our clients feel that we should have the best property in the neighborhood, but it must be a property that fits the neighborhood. You cannot gild the lily too much. You cannot create $300-per-month apartments in a $100-a-month neighborhood. But if you have $100 to $125 rentals in a typical $125 neighborhood you will be better off to offer real values at $125 and get satisfied tenants, than to bleed your building and get only $100 a month.[4]

Everett's emphasis on suitability to the neighborhood does not conceal the fact that he treats quality as a controllable variable on which, other things being equal, rents and, presumably, net income, will depend.

Under the heading of "Plan for operation and service," Atkinson and Frailey write,

The successful operation of an income property depends a lot on the quality of service rendered *in* the building. . . . When the manager prepares his program for the year, he must decide exactly how the building is going to be operated and how far he can go beyond bare necessity in offering those special services which may increase tenant satisfaction and thus have tangible influence on the maintenance of gross income. . . . He considers each possibility in relation to the effect it may have on securing tenants and keeping them happy . . . he tries to come out with the best possible combinations.[5]

A final quotation, this one from an article by W. A. P. Watkins, comes closer than any of the others cited to verifying our hypotheses:

[4] *Ibid.,* p. 13.
[5] *Fundamentals of Real Estate Practice,* pp. 192–93.

The same contractor [in Chicago] built three identical buildings in the same year in the mid-1920's. During the course of about four years in the early 1940's I was privileged to see the operating statements of all three buildings. To my mind, one building was being milked and was deteriorating much more rapidly than were the others. The second building, which had normal-to-good maintenance, was even in those days enjoying a $5 per month per apartment higher rent; the third building, which was superlatively maintained, was enjoying $2.50 more than the second building. . . . But when the operating statements were studied closely, it was clear that the middle building was consistently earning a higher net income than the neighbor which had better maintenance and higher rents, and that net income of both of the better-maintained buildings was substantially above that of the poorly maintained one. . . . From a management point of view, if you had bought the building which had been over-maintained and then let it slip slightly back toward the middle building which had an average maintenance more suitable to the neighborhood and the style of apartments, then you would have had a period of several years during which the operating expenses could have been slightly lower and the income could have been slightly higher.[6]

Much as these quotations may encourage one to accept the revenue-cost curve and rate-of-replacement hypotheses, they can never be regarded as real tests of validity. First of all, if one set out to disprove the hypotheses, he might be able to find quotations that argued for a different conclusion. Second, quotations may not accurately reflect behavior; only the actual behavior of firms can provide a valid test.

The Watkins quotation indicates one way in which the hypotheses might be tested against actual observations, for there are, in the larger American cities, many blocks of identical or virtually identical rental structures. By diligent fieldwork, one could probably assemble enough cases where operating outlays for identical structures have differed to test for the existence of a revenue-cost curve of the shape we have hypothesized. Observations for one year would certainly not suffice, however,

6 "Management as a Factor in Value," *Journal of Property Management,* September, 1956, pp. 18–19.

and collecting data for a five- or ten-year span would be difficult and expensive.

Two other obstacles are still more difficult to overcome. First, there is the problem of rate of replacement of structure: unless the buildings were all maintained in the same structural condition (a fact which would itself be difficult to establish), one could not treat rent and operating cost data as representing points on a single revenue-cost curve. Second, the results reported by Watkins depend peculiarly upon the implied irrationality or ignorance of two of the three owners: had they all been rational or fully informed, they would all have operated at the level of quality of the "middle" building, since that yielded the highest net income. If an extensive study produced more such instances of irrationality, it would verify the existence of revenue-cost curves while paradoxically casting doubt upon the ability of owners to discover or make use of them. Of course, one might uncover enough irrationality to trace out the curve without finding so much as to make it appear generally inoperative.

A much simpler plan of investigation would be to trace changes in operating outlays that take place in each of a number of individual buildings over a span of time in an effort to observe directly the response of gross rent to changes in variable inputs. But this kind of analysis would yield spurious results, for a given revenue-cost curve is, by hypothesis, a relationship which exists at a moment in time. If we attempt to measure it over a period of years, we shall observe changes in rent and cost that are likely to be due to shifts of the curve (as neighborhood, income, prices of inputs, etc., vary) rather than changes that represent movement along a given curve. Moreover, if we assume rational behavior and full information on the part of each owner, each would always be at his optimum level of quality of operation, and we could be certain that any changes in variable inputs we observed would necessarily be a response to changes in market conditions rather than a movement along a stable curve.

We conclude that the theory of housing operation and maintenance is not readily testable but that it is at least consistent with the description property managers themselves offer of their business conduct.

Evidence Concerning the Impact of Taxes

Can we find any evidence to support the conclusion that different real estate taxes will have different effects on the quality of operation or condition of structure of rental housing or on decisions concerning remodeling? Again, there are great obstacles. Our theory tells us what the differential effects of alternative real estate tax systems will be on rental structures within a given market (i.e., within a given metropolitan area). It does *not* predict differences in the effects of alternative taxes that would be observable between different markets (or metropolitan areas), where differences in the physical stock of housing are inevitably present and where the whole complex of nontax factors that affect the rental market for shelter are free to vary. Any attempt to test should therefore be confined to observations within a single market. The only opportunity for such a test would be an occasion on which a city switched from one real estate tax system to another. For example, if a city which had been taxing real estate on a gross-rent basis changed over to a tax on real estate net income or site value, while raising the same amount of revenue as before, our theory would predict a rise in quality of operation and rate of replacement in rental structures. By taking data before and after such a switch for a sample of structures, one might obtain observations with which to test the theory.

For better or worse, such changes in real estate tax systems in the United States have been infrequent. Moreover, historical instances are no help: the data cannot be gathered long after the event. Pittsburgh is the only large city in the United States in which the real estate tax base was ever radically altered from its traditional American form. True, a handful of single-tax colonies exist, but they help us not at all, since they are small villages or towns in which single-family homes predominate. They were planned and built as single-tax experiments and so cannot provide the sort of evidence one would look for on the occasion of a change-over.[7]

Unfortunately, as we shall see, Pittsburgh is no help either. The change in Pittsburgh was from tax No. 2, the traditional American levy, to a form halfway between tax No. 2 and tax No. 1, the site-value tax. But since our theory holds that neither Tax no. 2 nor Tax no. 1 has any direct effect on operating decisions or on decisions as to rate of replacement, the change at Pittsburgh would leave us only indirect income effects or effects on remodeling to look for. Moreover, the changeover in Pittsburgh took place gradually, so that the predicted effects, even if present, were spread out over many years.

On January 1, 1914, pursuant to an act of law signed by the Governor of Pennsylvania in 1913, Pittsburgh put into effect what came to be known as the "graded tax plan," an arrangement under which the city's tax on improvements is set at half the rate on site value.[8] The differential rates were put into effect step by slow step: in 1914 and 1915 the rate on improvements was reduced to 90 percent of the rate on the assessed value of land, in 1916 to 80 percent, in 1919 to 70 percent, in 1922 to 60 percent, and in 1925 to 50 percent. The ratio of the building rate to the land rate has remained at 1:2 ever since.[9] Even if one could collect enough data five decades after the event, the fact that the change in tax burden took place gradually over a period of eleven years would make

---

[7] The single-tax colonies are described in *Land-Value Taxation Around the World*, ed. by Harry Gunnison Brown and others (New York, Robert Schalkenbach Foundation, 1955). See chapters entitled "The Fairhope Colony" by C. A. Gaston, "The Three Ardens" by Donald Stephens, "Free Acres, New Jersey" by M. B. Thomson, and "The New England Enclaves" by Francis G. Goodale.

[8] Percy R. Williams, "Pennsylvania," in *ibid.*, pp. 93–105.

[9] Note that the graded tax plan does *not* result in site rents being taxed at twice the rate of building rents, since the heavy land tax depresses the capital value, and hence the assessed value of land, relatively more than the building tax depresses the capital value of buildings, even in the unlikely event that the building tax is not shifted to tenants.

it difficult to separate the influence of tax changes from other very important influences. Over the years a number of articles and monographs have discussed the Pittsburgh graded tax plan,[10] but a search through these reveals no data that could be used to test our theory.

The same law that put the graded tax plan into effect in Pittsburgh also set it in operation in Scranton, but again the gradual application of the plan and the lapse of time since it was adopted make it extremely doubtful whether one could use the Scranton case as a test. One more possibility in Pennsylvania remains: in 1951 the Governor signed into law an act allowing all third-class Pennsylvania cities (i.e., all cities except Philadelphia, Pittsburgh, and Scranton) the option of taxing land and buildings at different rates, without limitation as to the extent of the difference.[11] If any of these cities should choose to "untax" buildings, an opportunity might yet arise to test the theory within a single U.S. market.

An exemption and abatement along the lines of tax No. 6 has recently been operating in New York City, but the results are not significant for our purposes on account of the influence of rent control. The Housing and Redevelopment Board of the City of New York describes the tax benefits as follows:

In order to improve housing conditions, property owners can obtain tax benefits for alterations or improvements which eliminate fire or health hazards in apartment buildings occupied by three or more families for permanent residence purposes. The alterations or improvements include, among other improvements, installation of central or other approved heating where there is none presently existing and replacement of inadequate and obsolete sanitary facilities.

Section J41-2.5 of the Administrative Code, as added by local law 50 of 1960, provides the following tax benefits:

[10] See J. P. Watson, *The City Real Estate Tax in Pittsburgh*, Monograph No. 3 (Pittsburgh, Bureau of Business Research of the University of Pittsburgh, 1934); E. F. Daume, "The Graded Tax on Buildings," and T. C. McMahon, "Pittsburgh's Graded Tax on Buildings," in *Proceedings of the National Tax Association*, Twenty-second Annual Conference (Columbia, S.C., National Tax Association, 1930), pp. 140–50 and 134–40, respectively.

[11] Williams, in *Land-Value Taxation*, pp. 93–105.

1. Tax exemption for a period of 12 years on the increase in assessed valuation resulting from the improvement.

2. Abatement of the taxes equal to 75% of the reasonable costs of the improvement as estimated by the Housing and Redevelopment Board. This is to be in the form of 8⅓% abatement per year for a period of nine years. However, the abatement in any one year may not be greater than the year's tax.[12]

These benefits are, however, subject to a number of conditions, of which the most important are:

5. The tax benefits shall apply to any multiple dwelling only while subject to rent control [with exceptions then listed]. . . .

8. The present policy of the State Rent Commission is to order reductions in rent amounting to ⅔ of the tax abatement received by the owner where an increase in rent had been granted for the improvement for which tax abatement is obtained. This is an advantage to both the owner and the tenant because the total amount of benefits received by the owner as a result of the rent increase and tax abatement is greater than the amount of rent increase alone and the tenant pays a lower rent.[13]

This program exceeds tax No. 6 in scope, since it provides not only an exemption on the increased value created by the improvement but also a partial return of the cost of the improvement itself. The benefits offered with one hand are partly withdrawn by the other, however, since the landlord can increase his rent only to the extent allowed under rent control and then finds this increase reduced by an amount equal to two-thirds of the annual abatement. The net effect is that he can raise his rent by the amount allowable under rent control and, beyond that, collect one-third of the 8⅓ percent annual abatement. In addition, he is not taxed on the improvement for twelve years. The expectation that rent control might end would weaken rather than strengthen the incentive to use these provisions, since all the tax benefits terminate with decontrol.

[12] Housing and Redevelopment Board of the City of New York, *Instructions for Obtaining Tax Benefits for Housing Improvements* (undated), p. 1.
[13] *Ibid.*, pp. 2–3.

Thus, the New York City experience is not a valid test of the effectiveness of tax exemption and/or tax abatement in stimulating the improvement of rental housing in a competitive market. In conversation, New York City's Assistant Director of Assessment stated that the rent-control feature of the plan largely discouraged owners from participating.[14] He supplied a memorandum containing the data in Table 9.1 on the extent of the program.

TABLE 9.1

*Extent of Tax Benefits Enjoyed Pursuant to
Local Law 50 of 1960, During Tax Year 1961–62*

Number of parcels benefiting	922
Assessed value of parcels	$35,578,950
Exemption on same	$ 7,538,350
Certified cost of improvements	$ 9,945,447
Abatement based on cost	$ 828,785

In addition, he pointed out that (1) the Tax Commission had processed an additional 360 applications for the tax year 1962–63 and (2) the figures for 1961–62 include parcels that became eligible under earlier versions of the tax benefit plan running back to 1955.

It is difficult to evaluate the results. The assessed value listed above for 1961–62 represents 0.4 percent of the assessed value of all taxable apartment house structures in the city for that year, and the number of parcels represents 0.7 percent of the total number of such properties.[15] But this comparison is not the relevant one. Rather we should like to know the ratio of the value of benefiting properties to the value of that class of housing in which the provisions were intended to stimulate improvement. The latter comparison would undoubtedly result in much higher ratios. Moreover, the New York City program would probably be much more effective in the absence of rent control. On the other hand, however, the positive abatement included in New York's law is not a feature of tax No. 6 as defined. The net result of all these considerations is "No ver-

14 Interview with the late Alfred Jacobsen, June 8, 1962.
15 Citywide data for 1961–62 from City of New York, *Annual Report of the Tax Commission and the Tax Department as of June 30, 1961*, p. 46.

dict," with the possibility remaining that tax No. 6 could prove effective in a valid test.

A Study of Tax No. 2

Our theory has held that tax No. 2, the traditional American form, has no effect on operating decisions or decisions as to rate of replacement of structure. This conclusion is important and in itself may be worth testing. If the assessment process for tax No. 2 does not work in the manner described in Chapters 6 and 8, then our conclusions regarding the effects of that tax may be wrong.

On this point, a study of the relationship between assessments and quality of operation and condition of structure is needed. How might one go about it? The earlier discussion of possible evidence concerning the existence of revenue-cost curves suggests one answer. Again, the first line of approach would be the most useful: a group of identical buildings in the same neighborhood that yielded evidence concerning the shape of a revenue-cost curve would, ideally, also yield evidence concerning the relationship between assessed valuation and quality of operation and condition of structure. But as a practical matter we should not be too hopeful. Assessment practices in the United States are often deficient; one cannot attach much meaning to relatively small differences between the assessed valuation of two properties, yet the differences we are looking for are likely to be relatively small. With a large enough sample, one might still obtain reliable results, but in the nature of the case one is unlikely to have a large sample.

As an alternative, examination of identical buildings in different neighborhoods would be clearly useless not only because the revenue-cost curves could be expected to differ between neighborhoods but also because we would expect neighborhood to influence assessed value.

In addition to using statistical methods, one might attempt to get at the assessment process directly, by submitting questionnaires or hypothetical cases to a group of assessors and studying their replies. But since we are dealing with a public office in which the practice is known often to diverge widely from the theory, the reliability of results obtained in this way would be questionable.

A much easier task would be to study the relationship between tax No. 2 and housing rehabilitation. Buildings are quite likely to be re-assessed immediately after they have been rehabilitated, and it would be instructive to know how the new assessed valuation is related to various indicators of value such as gross rent and cost of rehabilitation. A group of case studies would probably throw much light on this matter.

It is important to note, however, that any conclusions regarding tax No. 2 based on evidence from one city will not necessarily be valid in another place or even at another time in the same place. Assessment is a complex legal and administrative procedure; there is no reason to attribute as much regularity to it as we are in the habit of attributing to private business behavior.

Evidence from Abroad

Real estate taxes other than tax No. 2 have been used quite extensively outside the United States. Once again, the best evidence to test our theory would be case-study data over periods in which the real estate tax system was changed from one which we would expect to be unfavorable to quality of operation and condition of structure to one that we would expect to be neutral, or vice versa.

In Australia and New Zealand, various federal, state, and national taxes upon the unimproved value of land have been used since around the turn of the century. Not all these are relevant for our purposes, however. For example, a federal land tax on unimproved value was levied in Australia from 1910 until 1952. New Zealand—a unitary state—introduced a national land tax in 1891 and has employed it ever since. Our interest, however, is limited to housing markets in which the tax on *improvements* changed. Therefore, the presence or absence of an overlying state or national tax on *unimproved* value is irrelevant. A large number of municipalities in which the relevant sort of change took place can be found in Australia, New Zealand, Canada, and the Union of South Africa. Almost all of them originally levied a tax on improvements of the sort we would expect to be unfavorable to quality of operation and subsequently completely untaxed improvements.

Unfortunately, we have been able to find in the available literature no useful evidence of the effects of any of these changes on the operation of rental housing—hardly surprising when one considers how specialized the data must be and how remote we are both in time and space from the events. The following paragraphs summarize very briefly the history of the movement to "untax" (or "derate") improvements in those countries where it has made any headway.[16] Our purpose is, first, to indicate where one might look for further evidence about the results, second, to put some historical flesh on the bare bones of "alternative tax types" we have been discussing.

In Australia local taxation is governed by state law. All six states of the Commonwealth either require or permit local units, at their option, to tax unimproved land value and exempt improvements. Before the movement for land-value taxation began, all localities taxed real estate on the annual value of land and improvements combined [17]—a system derived from the British "rates" and therefore comparable to our tax No. 5. The State of Queensland was the first to adopt land-value taxation for local units: the Valuation and Rating Act of 1890 excluded virtually all improvements from the tax base for local governments.[18] At various dates since then, all the other

[16] The principal sources for historical statements are *Land-Value Taxation*, chapters entitled "Australia" by E. J. Craigie, "New Zealand" by Rolland O'Regan, "The Union of South Africa" by Arthur W. Madsen, and "Canada" by Herbert T. Owens; Richard M. Bird, *The Taxation of Land Values in Canada and Australasia*, Master's Essay, Columbia University, 1960 (unpublished); and R. M. Haig, *The Exemption of Improvements from Taxation in Canada and the United States*, a report prepared for The Committee on Taxation of the City of New York (New York, 1915).

[17] *Land-Value Taxation*, p. 17.

[18] Bird, *Taxation of Land Values*, p. 68.

states, as well as the Capital Territory, have made the exemption of improvements either mandatory or permissible at local option, and more than half the local taxing units in the six states (as well as the Capital Territory itself) now exempt improvements entirely.[19] In Australia, therefore, hundreds of municipalities have switched from tax No. 5 to tax No. 1. But we would need case studies of rental structures in these markets for the period of changeover to obtain data to test our theory.

New Zealand presents much the same picture. In the early 1890s, localities taxed real property either on capital value or on annual value of site and improvements combined (taxes No. 2 and No. 5, respectively). Localities have had the power to change some rates from an improved to an unimproved value base since 1896 and have had the power to change all rates to the unimproved value base since 1911.[20] By 1954 a majority of the local authorities with taxing power had elected to exempt improvements from all rates.[21] But again we have found no data on the effects of rate changes that could be used to test our theory.

The Canadian case is quite different from that of Australia or New Zealand. Throughout Canada real property is taxed on its assessed capital value. But in many areas of western Canada, while land is taxed on its full assessed value, improvements are taxed on only part—at present usually one-half to three-quarters—of their assessed value.[22]

The control of taxing powers of localities is vested by the Canadian constitution entirely in the hands of the provincial legislatures. As early as 1874 the city of Nanaimo in British Columbia was able to grant complete exemption to improvements by virtue of a special charter. In 1892, British Columbia's General Municipal Act limited the assessment of improvements to 50 percent of full value and allowed total exemption of improvements at local option.[23] Between 1897 and 1913 Alberta,

19 *Land-Value Taxation.* Data are given state by state in a table on p. 17 of this reference. The table is undated, but the text implies that it was up to date at the time of writing. (The book was published in 1955.)
20 *Ibid.,* p. 31.   21 *Ibid.,* p. 32.   22 Bird, *Taxation of Land Values,* p. 85.
23 Haig, *Exemption of Improvements,* pp. 169–73.

Saskatchewan, and Manitoba adopted legislation providing for either total or partial exemption of improvements from local property taxes.[24]

Western Canada experienced a vigorous land boom in 1900–14, and it was during those years that improvements were progressively untaxed. By 1914 many cities were granting full exemption to improvements. But the land boom halted abruptly just before World War I broke out. Financial crises overtook many localities, and it was soon necessary to restore at least part of the value of improvements to the local tax rolls in all major cities.[25]

Thus, Canada provides many instances in which localities changed over from tax No. 2 to tax No. 1 (and almost as many in which they changed back again). In some cases, however, the shift occurred in several stages, which would make it difficult to study the effects even if one had the necessary data.

The shift away from taxation of improvements came somewhat later in the Union of South Africa than elsewhere in the British Commonwealth.[26] The Union consists of four provinces, each with an elected legislature in whose hands the (national) Union Parliament has left the control of local taxation. Real property is taxed as in the United States, on its assessed capital value rather than its annual value.

Originally all provinces required uniform rates of tax on land and improvements. The first change came in 1916, when the Transvaal required localities to tax land at a higher rate than improvements under a complex formula. Subsequently, the other three provinces adopted ordinances that granted localities wide freedom in choosing whether or at what rates to continue to tax improvements. Among the major cities of South Africa, Johannesburg has not taxed improvements since 1918–19, Pretoria taxes improvements at less than one-fifth the rate of land, Kimberley has not taxed improvements since 1945, Bloemfontein has exempted buildings since 1950, Durban

[24] *Land-Value Taxation*, pp. 63–67.   [25] *Ibid.*, pp. 70–74.
[26] The source for all information on the Union of South Africa is Madsen, in *Land-Value Taxation*.

taxes improvements at half the land rate, and Capetown continues to rate land and improvements equally.

Followers of Henry George (e.g., the contributors to *Land-Value Taxation Around the World*) are fond of citing the fact that in the British Commonwealth areas (except Canada), where improvements have once been "derated," there has been no tendency to return to the older equal, or "flat rating," system. They point out that in most cases the law provides that a reversion to the old system must take place if the voters in a municipality so decide in a referendum, and they are pleased to add that although many referendums have been held, very few have succeeded in overthrowing the Georgist reform, which must therefore be counted a success. There is an element of truth in this argument, but it must not be pushed too far, for a similar claim may be advanced on behalf of equal rating: in the United States the people are always free to adopt local option in these matters either by state legislation or state constitutional amendment, yet after eighty years of agitation almost no changes have been made in the traditional system. Perhaps legislative silence indicates popular consent. Yet the kernel of truth remains: the widespread use of local land taxation combined with full exemption of improvements at least suggests that there is nothing inherently unfeasible about tax No. 1.

As for the other real estate levies that have been used abroad, tax No. 5, is, of course, the form long applied in Great Britain. Our theory indicates that British "rates" would be unfavorable both to quality of operation and condition of structure were it not for the fact that assessed gross annual values of residential properties are frozen at their June, 1939, levels instead of reflecting actual performance. But even if current British experience were not thus modified, it would provide no way in which to test the theory of tax incidence, since it offers no examples of a changeover from one tax system to another.

It remains to mention the use of tax No. 3, a levy on gross rent, in various parts of Latin America. Shoup, Harriss, and Vickrey's detailed study of the revenue problem of the Federal

District of Venezuela mentions the use of taxes on the gross-rental value of real estate in both Buenos Aires and Montevideo.[27] In the Federal District of Venezuela itself, a tax on the annual rental value of real estate and on the capital value of unimproved land accounted for more than one-third of tax receipts in the second half of 1958.[28] The Venezuelan experience, like the British, apparently provides no way in which to test predictions concerning the effects of a tax with regard to quality of operation and condition of structure. It does, however, provide some insight into the administrative feasibility of tax No. 3. But this is a matter we shall deal with at greater length when we sum up the arguments for and against alternative real estate taxes in the concluding chapter.

[27] Carl S. Shoup, C. Lowell Harriss, and William S. Vickrey, *The Fiscal System of the Federal District of Venezuela: A Report* (New York, 1960), pp. 24–25.

[28] *Ibid.*, Table II-5, p. 15.

CHAPTER TEN

WEIGHING THE ALTERNATIVES

In choosing among possible systems of real estate taxation, one must obviously consider a great many criteria in addition to probable effects on maintenance and rehabilitation of urban rental housing. Instead of closing with a summary statement of these effects as analyzed in the central chapters of this study, we have thought it preferable to review a number of other criteria as well. Such a review cannot here be carried out at the level of detail employed in Chapters 2 through 8. It is to be hoped that the review will, nevertheless, assist the reader in seeing the policy problem in its whole complexity. So far as we know, no other discussion has attempted to bring together both the principal tax alternatives and the principal criteria of choice.

We propose to employ ten criteria in weighing the alternatives:
1. Operating effect.
2. Effect on rate of replacement of structure.
3. Remodeling effect.
4. New construction effect.
5. Other resource-allocating effects.
6. Effect on owner-occupied as compared with rental housing.
7. Relative administrative feasibility.
8. Relative stability of yield.
9. Relative adequacy of yield.
10. Equity.

Since the first four criteria were discussed at length in Chapters 7 and 8 and our conclusions summarized in Tables 7.1 and 8.1, only a few more words need be added. The effects of each tax alternative were described in those tables as being negative, neutral, or positive. Where a tax was found to be neutral, it was neutral with respect to a category of economic decisions and therefore neutral with respect to the allocation of resources to the corresponding category of activity. Where the tax had negative or positive effects, it altered the allocation of resources to a category of activity—by reducing it where the effect was negative or increasing it where the effect was positive. The unstated assumption behind the analysis was that we should all prefer neutral to negative effects but that some of us might, as a result of individual welfare preferences, prefer positive to neutral effects where they were feasible.

Our first four criteria do not, however, exhaust the resource-allocating effects of alternative real estate taxes. Those which remain to be dealt with we have brought together under the fifth heading, which follows.

Other Resource-Allocating Effects

The two principal matters now to be considered are, first, the effects of alternative tax systems on land use and, second, their effects on the utilization of the existing housing stock. On account of the long history of the single-tax controversy, a great deal has been written about the effects of real estate taxes on land use. We need not here go into such complex matters as which tax, under what assumptions covering the spatial pattern of demand for shelter, will have what effects on the location of economic activity. Instead, we shall concentrate on more general matters. The first of these is whether the various taxes discriminate among different land uses.

It has sometimes been asserted that a tax on the capital value of land discriminates against deferred uses. The assertion is based on the fact that a capital-value tax extracts payments from the owner who is holding property for a deferred use throughout the whole period before the use begins, these payments being based on the fact that the expected future income has a present value recognized in the market and therefore taxable. Then, when the deferred use finally commences, the tax bears on it in proportion to the income it yields, taxing it thereafter in the same proportion as it taxes other uses which yielded a level income over the whole period. When the whole period is considered, the deferred use will appear to have paid a higher proportion of its income in taxes than other uses which offered a level yield from the beginning.

Some writers have offered this argument as an objection to a capital-value tax on land. Pigou claimed that a tax on the actual annual rent of land is preferable in that it avoids such "discrimination" between immediate and deferred uses by not extracting payments from deferred uses until they begin to yield income. Pigou draws an analogy to investments in corporate shares and points out that in Britain

capital invested in securities is charged to income tax in respect of what it does, not in respect of what it might, yield. If a person has money in a company which is expected to prove profitable in the future, but which at present passes its dividends, he pays no tax, however high the capital value of the shares.[1]

The reference to British income tax suggests the basis for the claim of discrimination. The British, guided by the principle of taxing the fruit but not the tree, have traditionally declined to tax capital gains as income. The "discrimination" against deferred uses attributed to a tax on the capital value of land consists in the fact that it reaches the capital-gain element of the return as it accrues, while a tax on the actual annual rent allows the capital gain to escape entirely. If it is the practice, as it is in the United States, to treat capital gains as income, then there can be no objection to the land-value tax on this score, apart from the general objection that real estate taxes impose special burdens on one particular class of investment.

[1] Arthur Cecil Pigou, *The Policy of Land Taxation* (London, Longmans, Green, 1909), p. 17. I am indebted to Professor William S. Vickrey for clarifying several points in the analysis of Pigou's discussion of discriminatory taxation that follows.

Pigou has pointed out that there are not two but three possible bases on which to levy a tax on the public value of land. ("Public value," a term he borrowed from Marshall, denotes what is more commonly called "site value" or "unimproved value.") These bases are

1) the annual public value of land in the use to which it is actually put, as is done with the annual full value of land under the present English rating system; or 2) its annual public value in the use which would yield the largest immediate return—a value, in the case of uncovered land, equivalent to the rent for which it could be let with a covenant for immediate building; or 3) its capital public value.[2]

The difference between (1) and (2) is that under the former a vacant lot in a city is not taxed, while under the latter it is taxed on the income which it could earn if let for the most profitable immediate use.

In discussing the relative merits of these three tax bases, Pigou maintains not only that the second and third are inequitable by British standards—as already explained—but also that the alleged discrimination affects land use. Thus, he writes of the second basis that

an impost assessed on the public value of land in that use which would at the moment afford the largest profit differentiates against deferred uses; for it taxes them, when the whole period of their influence is considered, on more than their yield. It is, in fact, a discriminating tax upon deferred uses.

Against taxation of this kind there is a general *prima facie* presumption. That presumption may, however, in certain not improbable cases, be overcome. In the present instance the discrimination contemplated would probably increase somewhat the house accommodation available at the outskirts of towns.[3]

And concerning taxation on the third basis he adds

Taxation of capital value is a stronger measure. It works in the same direction as, but with greater force than, taxation of value in the immediately most profitable use.[4]

---

2 *Ibid.*, pp. 15–16.   3 *Ibid.*, p. 18.   4 *Ibid.*, p. 19.

This, however, is somewhat misleading. A land tax on either the capital value of land or on its annual rent in the immediately most profitable use would not affect the owner's choice among uses as compared with his choice if there were no tax, for a tax on either of these bases is equivalent to a lump-sum charge. No matter what actual use is made of the land, the tax base, and hence the tax, will remain unchanged. Hence, the tax cannot affect the owner's choice among uses.

In fact, the British "rates" (which strike the annual public value of land in the use to which it is actually put) and not the taxes on capital value or on annual value in the immediately most profitable use are "discriminating taxes," for in allowing the capital-gain element to escape tax completely, the British "rates" discriminate *in favor of* deferred uses as compared with immediate uses. Rates are *not* equivalent to a lump-sum tax: to take the simplest case, the tax can be avoided by leaving land vacant. Since the tax varies according to the use made of the land, it can affect the landowner's choice among possible uses. Pigou noticed the difference in effect between British rates and the two other varieties of land tax and came to the characteristically British conclusion that it was the non-British species that were "discriminating." On the contrary, the two non-British species would not alter land-use decisions from what they would be in the absence of land taxes, whereas British "rates" would do precisely that.

It must be noted that in another passage, Pigou recognizes that British rates are not entirely neutral to land-use decisions. He points out that if "we leave out of account the prospect of *changes* in the value of land, it is clear that our present system acts as a direct bounty on unremunerative uses of land," [5] for some owners, who might prefer a commercial use if there were no "rates," will choose a noncommercial use, such as a garden, when commercial uses are taxed but gardens are not. This observation must lead us to add that British rates discriminate not only in favor of deferred but also in favor of noncommercial uses.

If one wished to encourage the retention of open spaces

5 *Ibid.,* p. 16.

within cities, he might therefore prefer "rates" to the two other forms of land tax. On the other hand, vacant land also imposes costs upon a city in the form of both wasted public services and higher private costs of transportation. On the whole, it would appear that the provision of open space is best accomplished directly by zoning and the creation of parks. Tax incentives do not determine land use with the certainty necessary for effective long-range city planning.

In any case, arguments to the effect that some form of land tax will cause too much urban congestion should be regarded skeptically. Most of them completely overlook the general-equilibrium nature of the land-use problem: people moving into one block necessarily move out of another. Then, too, the term "congestion" is not always carefully defined. Construction of more buildings means greater density of structures, but if the population does not increase as a consequence, it also means a lower density of people per unit of structure, which is just the opposite of congestion.[6]

We may now apply our conclusions concerning land-use effects to the family of alternative real estate taxes. To simplify the discussion, we shall assume that there are no improvements to land such as grading and draining, so that we may equate the whole rent of land with its annual unimproved, or site, value.

Tax No. 1 is levied on the assessed capital value of a site. As argued above, such a tax does not affect the choice among possible land uses. On the same grounds, tax No. 2, the traditional American levy on combined value of site and improvements, in so far as it taxes land, is neutral as among possible land uses.

Tax No. 3 is based on actual gross rent. In so far as it taxes

[6] That Haig understood this distinction is clear from the following quotation concerning the effects of taxing sites and untaxing buildings in Vancouver:
"The movement toward apartment building is strong and the tax system may be partly responsible for this; but, if so, it is probably not the most important factor. These are indications of a tendency toward increased congestion per acre. So far as buildings are made cheaper because of the reduced carrying charge, the exemption of improvements undoubtedly operates to reduce congestion per room." Robert M. Haig, *The Exemption of Improvements from Taxation in Canada and the United States*, a report prepared for the Committee on Taxation of the City of New York (New York, 1915), p. 273.

the gross rent of land, it is similar to Pigou's tax on public value in the actual use to which land is put, since the gross rent of land, as reached by tax No. 3, is precisely the same as its net rent, or annual value. Thus, tax No. 3 would encourage both deferred and noncommercial uses.

Tax No. 4, based on the net income of real estate, would, like taxes No. 2 and 3, reach both land and buildings. Its effect on land would be similar to that of tax No. 3 or of Pigou's tax on actual public annual value, since the net income from land is exactly equal to its gross rent, or annual public value.

Although tax No. 4 would resemble tax No. 3 in the direction of its effect on land-use decisions, it is important to note a difference which arises between the two cases because they do not apportion the burden in the same ratio between land and improvements. The tax base in land would be identical for both levies, since the gross rent of land equals its net income. But the gross-rent tax would have a much larger base in building rent than would the net-income tax. Therefore, for equal yield, the rate of tax No. 3 would be much lower than the rate of tax No. 4. Consequently, the latter would take a larger proportion of aggregate land rent than the former and a smaller proportion of aggregate gross building rent.

The difference in the division of a given burden has two results. First, since the portion of either tax falling on buildings is ultimately passed on to tenants with "negative" effects on resource allocation to new construction or remodeling, other things being equal, we would expect the negative effects to be stronger in the case of tax No. 3.

The second result concerns land-use effects. Since the burden on land rent would be relatively heavier in the case of tax No. 4, that tax would have a more powerful effect on land use than would tax No. 3—the effect in question being to encourage deferred and noncommercial uses.

Tax No. 5, the British "rates," would, as already argued, also encourage deferred and noncommercial uses. (The argument, of course, has referred to the pure theory of British "rates," not the actual practice as altered by infrequent or imperfect assessments, exemptions or partial exemptions for certain uses, and so on.) Although tax No. 5 parallels taxes No. 3 and No. 4 in its effects on land use, it differs from both in the division of total burden between land and improvements. It differs from tax No. 3, the gross-rent levy, in being theoretically a *net*-rent tax; as explained in Chapter 6, the ratable value of residential property is its gross annual value less a statutory percentage deduction allowed for expenses. This means that the tax base is smaller and the rate therefore higher under the British system than would be the case with a gross-rent levy such as tax No. 3. Consequently, British "rates" take a higher portion of land rent and a smaller proportion of gross building rent than would the gross-rent tax. Yet "rates" do not divide the burden the same way a true net-income tax would, for "rates" are levied on what might be called "statutory net" rather than "actual net": first, because they are levied against an assessed rather than an actual base; second, because no matter how low assessed gross rent falls, statutory net rent never falls below 60 percent of gross—40 percent being the highest allowable deduction for expenses.

The resource-allocating effects on taxes No. 6 and No. 7 depend, as do many of the characteristics of those levies, upon the basic tax with which they are combined. Nothing more need be added here.

We must now consider the manner in which the alternative taxes affect the use of the existing housing stock. As Herbert W. Robinson has shown, a tax which treats vacant and occupied improvements alike has different effects from one which taxes occupied improvements but exempts vacant ones.[7] For this purpose we have to assume, as we have not done in previous chapters, that there is a cyclical element in the demand for housing. Then to tax occupied improvements but not vacant improvements is to convert the property tax from a fixed to a variable expense with respect to occupancy. In the short run,

[7] "A Note on Unoccupied Houses," *Review of Economic Studies*, June, 1939, pp. 209–14.

in which we assume a fixed housing stock, this would hurt tenants by diminishing the supply of housing in case demand fell off, for the landlord, if he can do no better, will continue to accept tenants only as long as, taken together, they pay rents in excess of his variable costs of operation.

If we raise the level of variable costs by making taxes variable with respect to occupancy, we raise the minimum rent at which owners will continue to operate and increase the amount of usable space that will be boarded up in hard times. We conclude that in the short run the exemption of vacant improvements would cause a misallocation of resources, for housing services which consumers would willingly pay the marginal cost of producing are not produced on account of the tax attached to them. This effect can be avoided either by taxing vacant as well as occupied improvements or by exempting both from tax.

Applying these results to the alternative taxes, we find that tax No. 2, on the combined value of land and improvements, is collected on vacant as well as occupied premises and is therefore neutral with respect to boarding up. Tax No. 1, on site value, exempts all improvements and is therefore also neutral. Tax No. 4, the net-income tax, is likewise neutral, since it varies with profits, not with occupancy or rental income. Tax No. 3, on gross rent, and tax No. 5, the British "rates," are the only ones among the basic types that would encourage boarding up. Tax No. 3 would do so because it is collected from the owner if he has tenants but not if he does not. Tax No. 5 would do so because it is collected from tenants and therefore raises the gross level of payments needed to cover a given level of the landlord's variable costs. In both cases the owner will shut down in hard times when gross payments by tenants no longer cover his variable costs plus taxes. Hence, whether collected from landlord or tenant, a tax based on gross rent will encourage boarding up.

Tax No. 7, a penalty levied against substandard buildings, could also encourage boarding up, as was pointed out in Chapter 7. Tax No. 6, however, a tax abatement, simply preserves the characteristics, in this regard, of whatever basic tax it is combined with.

One point remains to be made in connection with resource-allocating effects. We assume that revenues are to be held constant as we compare alternative taxes. This means that a tax which exempts vacant land and improvements must tax occupied land and improvements by just that much more. But all taxes on improvements have unfavorable new construction and remodeling effects, and some of them have unfavorable effects on rate of replacement and quality of operation as well. Other things being equal, we would expect these effects to be more unfavorable when vacant land and improvements are exempt than when they are taxed.

Our conclusions concerning "other resource-allocating effects" of the alternative taxes are summarized in Table 10.1.

TABLE 10.1

Other Resource-Allocating Effects

Tax Type	Land-Use Effects	Housing-Use Effects	Other Effects
No. 1 (capital value of site)	Neutral among all uses	Neutral (exempts all improvements)	. . .
No. 2 (assessed value of land and improvements)	Neutral among all uses	Neutral (taxes vacant and occupied property equally)	. . .
No. 3 (gross rent)	Favors deferred and noncommercial uses	Favors boarding up	Exemption of vacant property increases burden on occupied
No. 4 (net income)	Favors deferred and noncommercial uses	Neutral (tax ceases before boarding-up point is reached)	Exemption of unprofitable uses increases burden on profitable
No. 5 (British "rates")	Favors deferred and noncommercial uses	Favors boarding up	Exemption of vacant property increases burden on occupied
No. 6 (abatement)	. . .	. . .	. . .
No. 7 (penalty)	. . .	May encourage boarding up	. . .

*Effect on Owner-Occupied as Compared
with Rental Housing*

We consider it desirable that the real estate tax not discriminate between owner-occupied and rental housing. Tax No. 1, on site value, is nondiscriminatory in principle and so meets this test. In practice, however, it might have the same drawbacks as mentioned below for tax No. 2.

Tax No. 2, on the combined value of site and improvement, provides the desired neutral treatment, with some qualifications. The qualifications are, first, that "homestead exemptions" in some states allow home-owners but not renters a partial reduction in assessments and, second, that regardless of equal assessment provisions in the law, some localities assess owner-occupied homes at a lower ratio to full value than other properties, including rental housing.[8]

Tax No. 3, on gross rent, could be applied to owner-occupied houses only through special provisions. The tax authorities would have to assess imputed gross rent as a tax base for all owner-occupied properties. This procedure would open the way for inequality of treatment (favorable to owners) at least as great as that prevailing under tax No. 2.

Tax No. 4 on real estate net income raises even greater difficulties than tax No. 3 in connection with owner-occupied properties. Home-owners and other owner-occupants would have to be taxed on the basis of an imputed net income from their properties. Over the course of the business cycle, the net income from rental properties is, or at any rate can be, highly variable. Would imputed net incomes of owner-occupied properties be allowed to vary as widely? If not, the tax burden on home-owners would rise sharply during a depression. The complications involved in bringing a net-income tax to bear equitably on owner-occupied properties are formidable, indeed.

8 For example, in New York City the assessment to sales-price ratio for all properties sold in 1950 was 0.87 and for all properties other than one- and two-family houses it was 0.98, while for one-family houses it was only 0.67. Data are from Robert M. Haig and Carl S. Shoup, *The Financial Problem of the City of New York: A Report to the Mayor's Committee on Management Survey* (New York, June, 1952), Table 37, p. 134, and text, p. 135.

Tax No. 5, the British "rates," is levied on assessed rather than actual rentals. In theory it meets the test of neutrality as between owners and renters.

Whether taxes No. 6 and No. 7, an abatement and a penalty, respectively, would treat owners and renters alike depends partly upon what basic tax they are combined with and partly upon a social decision as to whether they *ought* to apply to owner-occupied housing. Although owner-occupants of sub-standard homes might welcome the abatement incentive of tax No. 6, they are unlikely to applaud the penalties of tax No. 7. Doubtless they will never be required to bear them: forcing slum-owners to improve their properties is quite a different matter politically from compelling home-owners to do so.

Table 10.2 summarizes our discussion of the renter-owner criterion.

TABLE 10.2

The Renter-Owner Criterion

Tax Type	Effect on Owner-Occupied as Compared with Rental Housing
No. 1 (capital value of site)	Neutral
No. 2 (assessed value of land and improvements)	Neutral (in law, but favors owners in practice)
No. 3 (gross rent)	Requires special provisions
No. 4 (net income)	Requires special provisions
No. 5 (British "rates")	Neutral
No. 6 (abatement)	Uncertain
No. 7 (penalty)	Uncertain

Relative Administrative Feasibility

Administrative feasibility is an important criterion for choice among alternative taxes. It is a concept which seems plain enough at first but is, when one comes down to it, exceedingly difficult to define. We propose to get around the difficulty by inserting the word "relative." We then take as our standard of feasibility the traditional American tax on the assessed value of land and improvements combined, and the discussion narrows to whether each alternative is more or less difficult than that to administer. According to the received view, the American tax is administratively feasible as a local levy.[9] Hence, we have a good reference point for comparisons.

The administrative feasibility of tax No. 1 is a matter of debate. Some analysts are convinced that it would be much more difficult to assess unimproved land values than to assess land and improvement value combined, as is done with tax No. 2. For example, Ursula K. Hicks writes, "Fundamentally objective valuations must be based on selling prices; in a developed country independent selling prices for uncovered (and a fortiori undeveloped) sites are not available in sufficient numbers to serve." [10] Ernest Fisher goes even farther: he maintains that the value of a site and the value of the improvements on it cannot be disentangled, even theoretically.[11] If this proposition is accepted, then a land-value tax is certainly not administratively feasible. But, in company with most other writers on the topic, we reject the proposition.

The fact remains that in developed regions, sales of unimproved sites are less numerous than sales of improved ones, so that the market information needed to work out accurate assessments would be less plentiful for tax No. 1 than for tax No. 2. The only question is, would it be so scarce as to make accurate assessment very difficult? It is at this point that one reaches the bedrock of disagreement. When Pigou took up the question half a century ago, he began by saying, "The problem

[9] This should not, however, be taken to imply that it is always well-administered. The point emerges clearly in W. J. Shultz and C. L. Harriss' textbook. Concerning "the future of the property tax," the authors write, "Four considerations favor continued large-scale use of property taxation by local governments: . . . 2) the tax as it applies to real estate can be administered effectively, and even well, by local governments . . . major arguments against heavy use of the tax are: 1) administration by many local units is still distressingly bad." *American Public Finance* (7th ed., Englewood Cliffs, N.J., Prentice-Hall, 1959), p. 405.

[10] *Public Finance* (London, Cambridge University Press, 1947), p. 202. A somewhat similar position is taken by John R. Hicks in "Unimproved Value Rating—The Case of East Africa," reprinted in his *Essays in World Economics* (New York, Oxford University Press, 1959), and by the two authors together in their *Report on Finance and Taxation in Jamaica* (Kingston, Jamaica, Government Printer, 1955), Chap. X, "The Question of Unimproved Value Rating."

[11] Ernest M. Fisher and Robert M. Fisher, *Urban Real Estate* (New York, Holt, 1954), pp. 54–57.

thus suggested is not one upon which the opinion of an academic writer can carry any weight." [12] Undeterred, he pursued the matter a bit further. He noted that the majority of the Royal Commissioners on Local Taxation had decided that separate valuation of sites would be "attended with considerable uncertainty, complication and expense" [13] but also that the signatories of the minority report came to the opposite conclusion.[14] After pointing out that New York City had recently (1904) and at very slight expense adopted the practice of separately assessing land and improvements and that assessment of unimproved land values was recognized practice in Australasia, Pigou concluded by saying, "It would seem that the burden of proof must lie upon those who hold that the difficulties and expense of valuation are . . . sufficient to outweigh the general considerations in favour of the taxation of the public value of land." [15] One must be careful to notice that this is not a dismissal of the "difficulties," for Pigou attaches considerable weight to "the general considerations in favour of the taxation of the public value of land."

Concerning the administration of tax No. 1, we accept these propositions: (1) the separate assessment of land values is feasible, since it has long been the practice in several parts of the world; and (2) the separate assessment of land values cannot be easier and is likely to be somewhat more difficult than the assessment of the value of land and improvements combined. This means that tax No. 1 must be ranked as relatively more difficult to administer than tax No. 2.

So far as ease of administration is concerned, a gross-rent tax, like tax No. 3, has both advantages and disadvantages compared with tax No. 2. In every city some properties are owner-occupied, some rented. In dealing with the latter, a gross-rent tax has certain administrative advantages: first, the

12 *Land Taxation*, p. 14.

13 Quoted by Pigou from United Kingdom Royal Commission on Local Taxation, *Separate Report on Urban Rating and Site Values*, Final Report, Cd. 638 (1901), p. 43.

14 *Ibid.*, p. 169.   15 *Land Taxation*, p. 15.

assessment apparatus is eliminated; second, the tax can accurately reflect year-to-year market changes, whereas a tax on assessed value tends to lag; and third, since the tax base is a market-determined price rather than an administratively estimated one, there is less danger of systematic under- or overtaxation of one class of property as compared with another.

As Shoup, Harriss, and Vickrey's study of the finances of the Federal District of Venezuela shows, however, a gross-rent tax is not without its own administrative difficulties, even as it is applied to rental rather than owner-occupied properties.[16] Prominent among these are the following:

1. The services provided by landlord to tenant vary widely, sometimes including and sometimes omitting furniture, utilities, and various elements of maintenance and operating costs. Therefore, it is inequitable simply to levy the tax on contract rent; a good deal of adjustment is needed to put all taxpayers on a uniform basis.

2. Taxpayers would be expected to report their gross-rent receipts annually, and principally on the basis of this information would tax bills be rendered. This amounts to self-assessment, absent in the case of tax No. 2, and raises the specter of tax evasion, auditing procedures, and other unpleasantnesses associated with the income tax.

3. The tax administrator would have to make or obtain periodic physical surveys of his jurisdiction and keep careful records of the existence and extent of all properties in order to make sure that none escape the tax. These tasks are not unlike some of those required for an assessed-value levy such as tax No. 2.

Finally, of course, owner-occupied properties, a class including many of the largest business properties as well as many homes, would have to be taxed on the basis of an imputed gross rental. This would not be an easy operation and would reopen the door to the time lags and inequities of treatment

---

[16] Carl S. Shoup, C. Lowell Harriss, and William S. Vickrey, *The Fiscal System of the Federal District of Venezuela: A Report* (New York, 1960), Chap. IV.

that a pure gross-rent tax would have been expected to minimize.

On the whole, tax No. 3 seems to add as many difficulties as it eliminates and can accordingly be ranked as about the equal of tax No. 2 on administrative feasibility.

Tax No. 4, a net-income tax on real estate, would be very difficult to administer. First, there is the problem of how to deal with owner-occupied properties. Assessing an imputed net income is a less satisfactory solution here than assessing imputed gross rent would be in connection with tax No. 3. This is so because net income is a residual and therefore more volatile than gross rent. The likelihood of assessing it accurately (i.e., equal to what it would be if the property were actually let) for any one property in any one year is accordingly much less. In fact, it is difficult to imagine either that a government would attempt to establish or that owner-occupants would be willing to pay an assessed net-income tax. Therefore, a net-income tax would probably apply only to income properties, while the rest would be taxed on some wholly other basis, which would raise further administrative problems, in addition to serious issues of equity.

But even the application of the tax to rental properties would be difficult. Like tax No. 3, the net-income tax would be self-assessed, but in this case the authorities could not easily check the taxpayer's accuracy. Unless federal or state income-tax returns could be resorted to, the tax collector could verify accuracy only by a complete audit of the taxpayer's business records. Even state income-tax returns on real estate enterprises have been found by Arthur D. Sporn to be highly unreliable.[17] Auditing is, in any case, very difficult because ownership of rental real estate is very widely distributed among smallholders, who are not renowned for record-keeping. Accurately checking their accounts would often be exceedingly troublesome, if not impossible. Moreover, the tax would tempt owners into evasion or avoidance through such devices as ex-

[17] "Empirical Studies in the Economics of Slum Ownership," *Land Economics,* November, 1960, pp. 333–40.

pensing capital improvements or taking profits out in the form of a salary or of excessive depreciation. It is hard to imagine that many small properties would be found to yield any taxable income whatever. Yet even for large properties, as John A. Zangerle has pointed out, the determination of net income is perplexing.[18] There is no escaping the conclusion that tax No. 4 would be much more difficult to administer than the traditional American real estate tax.

Tax No. 5, the British "rates," involves valuation of all properties just as does the American tax No. 2. But the British assess the annual value (i.e., rent) rather than the capital value. Since more properties are rented than are sold each year, there is more evidence on which to base rental than capital-value assessments. This might be supposed to make the British system easier to administer than the American (assuming, which is not the case in Britain, that tax No. 5 were to be uniformly levied on a *current* rather than a *historical* base). But we must offset against this the fact that owner-occupied properties have to be assessed on the basis of an *imputed* annual value under tax No. 5. In many cases these assessments will never be put to the test of a market transaction.

In addition, the transition from gross annual value to net (or "ratable") value would be administratively difficult if one made any real attempt to arrive at a net basis. The British get around this problem by applying a rule of thumb to move from gross to net, with the final effect of taxing not true net annual value but a base consisting of a fraction of gross annual value. All things considered, the administrative feasibility of tax No. 5 is about the same as that of tax No. 2.

Tax No. 6, an abatement, would add another program to be administered in addition to the basic tax with which it was combined. But one must offset against this the fact that some assessments (or other base) would be at least temporarily fixed by tax No. 6, which would tend to reduce the adminis-

18 "Taxing Real Estate on Its Net Income," in *Property Taxes*, a symposium (New York, Tax Policy League, Inc., 1940), pp. 205–17.

trative burden. On balance, it seems probable that tax No. 6 would be harder to administer than tax No. 2.

Tax No. 7, a penalty, is necessarily more difficult to administer than any of the basic taxes with which it might be combined, since it would add further steps to whatever administrative process the basic tax required.

Tax No. 7, however, raises questions of a more general nature, which are perhaps best treated at this point. In previous chapters it was shown that the effects of tax penalties are uncertain and may sometimes be perverse. One might, therefore, argue that their intended objectives can better be achieved by the application of housing codes, for a system of penalties cannot be put into effect unless society specifies precisely a set of technical characteristics of housing which constitute a minimum acceptable standard above which the penalty will not apply. But if such a set can be specified, then it can be made part of the code standard which buildings are required by law to come up to as a condition of operation. Although the enforcement of codes has often been lax in the United States, there is no presumption that the enforcement of tax penalties would be any less so. Nor would it be easy to predict just what effects penalties would have, even if enforced.

The same objection cannot be made to a tax abatement, for an abatement is permissive only. It is merely an invitation to improve. It cannot have perverse effects. It can, but need not, specify particular objectives and hence is not administratively as close to a housing code as is a tax penalty system. Its goal is a general improvement, either through provision of more operating services or by better adaptation of the standing stock to changing patterns of demand. The latter objective, at least, could not possibly be attained by means of the necessarily formal legal provisions and processes of a housing code and its enforcement.

On the other hand, there are valid arguments favoring the penalty tax approach,[19] for a penalty offers a degree of flexi-

19 I am indebted to Professor William S. Vickrey for pointing these out to me.

bility, where a code requirement is absolute. The practical consequence in code formulation is often either to tolerate preexisting conditions and require conformity only in new construction or else to set the code standard low enough so that few are compelled to take costly action to conform. As compared with such an outcome, penalties might be preferable. If it is undesirable to compel compliance when compliance would be unusually costly, the penalty approach allows the owner to avoid that cost and pay the penalty instead. One could set higher standards with a penalty than with a code and still avoid imposing excessive hardship. Moreover, instead of granting outright exemptions to preexisting noncomplying uses, one could keep them under a moderate pressure to comply or to raze.

From these arguments we conclude not that the penalty tax approach is faulty but that it can be more appropriately considered in connection with the problem of housing codes than as a separate tax measure. Within the scope of this book, however, we cannot venture into that area.

Table 10.3 summarizes our conclusions on administrative feasibility.

TABLE 10.3

Administrative Feasibility Criterion

Tax Type	Administrative Feasibility as Compared with Tax No. 2
No. 1 (capital value of site)	Probably somewhat harder to administer
No. 2 (assessed value of land and improvements)	. . .
No. 3 (gross rent)	About the same
No. 4 (net income)	Much harder to administer
No. 5 (British "rates")	About the same
No. 6 (abatement)	Probably somewhat harder to administer
No. 7 (penalty)	Harder to administer

Revenue Criteria—Stability of Yield

Revenue criteria are highly important in weighing alternative real estate taxes at this date. American cities are financially hard-pressed. The growth of population and the demand for more extensive and higher quality public services have built up pressure for ever more local public expenditures. Finding revenue has not been easy. The local property tax remains by far the largest source of funds. As Table 10.4 shows, in 1960 property taxes yielded $15.8 billion of local revenue, providing 43 percent of all local revenues (including all nontax receipts), and 87 percent of all local *tax* receipts.

TABLE 10.4

Local Government Revenues

	Amount ($ millions)			Percent of Total Local Revenue [a]		
	1940	1950	1960	1940	1950	1960
Intergovernmental	1,932	4,428	9,953	25	28	27
From federal government	278	211	592	4	1	2
From states	1,654	4,217	9,361	21	26	25
Revenue from own sources	5,792	11,673	27,209	75	72	73
Taxes	4,497	7,984	18,081	58	50	49
Property	4,170	7,042	15,798	54	44	43
Sales and gross receipts	130	484	1,339	2	3	4
Income	19	71	254	. . .	, . .	. . .
All other taxes	178	387	690	2	2	2
Charges and miscellaneous general revenue	510	1,602	4,831	7	10	13
Utility revenue	704	1,808	3,613	9	11	10
Liquor store revenue	13	94	136	. . .	1	. . .
Insurance trust revenue	68	185	549	1	1	1
Total local revenue	7,724	16,101	37,163	100	100	100

[a] Details may not add to totals because of rounding.
Sources:
U.S. Department of Commerce, Bureau of the Census: for 1960 data, *Governmental Finances in 1960*, Table 1; for earlier years, *1957 Census of Governments*, Vol. IV, No. 3, Table 6.

In comparing alternative taxes, we shall consider first the stability and then the adequacy of probable revenue yield. Stability is important because local governments cannot readily borrow to meet operating budgets. We shall narrow the discussion to stability of the tax *base*. The yield could usually be held constant over the course of a business cycle by making the *rate* vary inversely with changes in the base. Taxpayers, however, are likely to resist, at least during the phase when rates have to rise. Stability of the tax base (or of revenue, given constant rates) is therefore the matter at issue. We shall take the base of tax No. 2, the traditional American levy, as a standard for purposes of comparison, since the yield stability of this tax has often been described as one of its virtues.

The stability of the base tax No. 2 is not difficult to demonstrate. It is a peculiar quality, however, for it depends importantly on the fact that assessments do not fully reflect the cyclical swing of real estate market values. When the market rises rapidly, assessors tend to stay below full market-value assessments; when the market falls rapidly, they also avoid an equally rapid reduction of assessments. The result is not just a lag of changes in assessment behind changes in market value but a marked damping of the amplitude of the former as compared with the latter. Real estate owners, during a depression at any rate, find this highly inequitable. But since the sluggishness of response by assessors is virtually built into the system, we will accept it as a fact and measure the stability of tax No 2. by the stability of actual assessment rather than of assessments corrected to full value. For this purpose we have chosen data on the assessed value of taxable real estate in New York City.[20]

The New York City data show a rise of 127 percent from 1920 to the peak in 1932, followed by a decline of 15 percent to the low point in 1935 or of 19 percent to the still lower level of wartime 1944–45. From that date to 1950–51, taxable assessed value then rose 16 percent.[21] From 1944–45 to 1960–61, assessed values rose 58 percent. In order to compare the stability of other taxes with that of tax No. 2, we shall measure the amplitude of change of other appropriate time series over the same period, or as much of it as we have data for.

To compare the stability of the base of tax No. 1 on site value with that of tax No. 2, we can make use of New York City data on the assessed value of taxable land.[22] From 1920 to the 1931 peak, land values rose 96 percent. From that point

20 See Appendix B, Table B.1.

21 The failure of these swings to equal the amplitude of the market price cycle can be inferred from data on assessment-sales ratios for 1938–50 in Haig and Shoup, *Financial Problem of City of New York*, Fig. 10, p. 187.

22 See Appendix B, Table B.1.

to the 1936 low, they declined 20 percent, and to the 1946–47 trough, 29 percent. From 1946–47 to 1960–61, land values then rose 23 percent. These changes are of about the same magnitude as those for the base of tax No. 2, the principal point of difference being that land values fell further than the land and improvements aggregate over the course of the depression and war and recovered less rapidly afterwards. These comparisons, and other ones below, are summarized in Table 10.5.

Obviously, the New York City data by themselves are an insufficient basis on which to draw firm conclusions. Unfortunately, there are no nationwide time series on real estate values sufficiently reliable to make use of.[23]

To estimate the probable stability of tax No. 3 on gross rent we have two gross-rent series.[24] The first, covering nationwide gross rent (exclusive of the imputed rental value of owner-occupied business and farm property) is assembled from data for 1929–51, published by the U.S. Department of Commerce. This nationwide series displays a much more pronounced postwar growth trend than do the New York City assessment data, no doubt partly because rent control has lasted longer in New York than elsewhere and has been more effective there because the city is predominantly a rental rather than an ownership market. Other factors, such as differences in rate of population growth, may have entered as well. In any case, rent control would seem to invalidate a postwar comparison between New York and national data. No such objection can

[23] The estimates developed by Raymond Goldsmith for the period 1896–1949 are not useful, because his series on the value of land is derived by applying quite stable estimated ratios of land to building value to various series on the value of structures. In comparing changes in land value to changes in the value of land and structures combined, one would therefore be performing a meaningless operation. Of course, the fact that Goldsmith, after studying the evidence, uses rather stable ratios of land value to structure value suggests that, indeed, the two series may track rather closely. But the question cannot be answered reliably without a detailed study that falls outside the scope of this paper. See Raymond W. Goldsmith, Dorothy S. Brady, and Horst Mendershausen, *A Study of Saving in the United States* (Princeton, N.J., Princeton University Press, 1956), Vol. III, Table W-1 and Notes, pp. 14–15. The ratios of land value to building value used in deriving land value estimates for Table W-1 are given in Tables B-50 and B-51, Vol. II, pp. 397–98.

[24] See Appendix B, Table B.2.

TABLE 10.5

Comparison among Tax Bases for Stability

(percent change during period indicated)

Period	Tax No. 2 (N.Y.C. Assessed Values)	Tax No. 1 (N.Y.C. Assessed Values)	Tax No. 3		Tax No. 4	
			Nationwide Gross Rent	N.Y.C. Sample Gross Rent	Nationwide Net Rent	N.Y.C. Sample Net Rent
1920–32	+127	...	...	...	...	...
1920–29	...	...	...	+ 36	...	...
1920–31	...	+ 96	...	...	...	...
1929–35	− 15	...	...	...	...	...
1929–34	...	...	− 36	...	− 55	...
1929–35	...	...	...	− 40	...	...
1929–44/5	− 19	...	...	...	...	...
1929–46/7	...	− 29	...	...	...	...
1925/9–40/4	...	...	...	...	...	− 49
1944/5–50/1	+ 16	...	...	...	...	...
1944/5–60/1	+ 58	...	...	...	...	...
1935–50	...	...	...	+ 43	...	...
1946/7–60/1	...	+ 23	...	...	...	...
1934–51	...	...	+196	...	+316	...
1940/4–50	...	...	...	...	...	+ 27

be made to a comparison covering the depression period. Examining the decline from the 1929 peak to the depression trough for both series, we find that New York City assessed values declined only 15 percent (1929 to 1935), while nation-wide gross rents fell 36 percent (1929 to 1934). Comparisons are again assembled in Table 10.5.

For a second comparison between tax No. 3 and tax No. 2, we make use of the series on gross rent developed by Leo Greb-ler [25] from his study of 581 New York City properties.[26] His data cover the years 1900 through 1950. Since his study was limited to New York City properties, his results reflect the existence of rent control. They eliminate that difficulty, however, at the expense of introducing others: Grebler's sample could not be scientifically designed to be representative of the New York market as a whole, for he had to rely on cases that had good, continuous accounting records. Whether the sample accurately represents the movement of the market as a whole is not known. It certainly cannot display a growth trend of the sort associated with sheer growth in number or size of properties.

The Grebler series rose 36 percent from 1920 to 1929, fell 40 percent to a low point in 1935, then rose 43 percent by 1950. The comparable movement of the assessed-value series was much greater from 1920 to 1932, when it rose 127 percent, but much smaller from 1932 to 1944–45, when it fell only 19 percent, and from that date to 1950–51, when it rose only 16 percent (see Table 10.5). The greater increase in assessed value during the 1920s is undoubtedly explained by the real estate boom of that decade, the growth aspect of which, as we pointed out, is not reflected in an "experience of average prop-erty" series like Grebler's. For the period of the 1930s and 1940s, when new construction was at a minimum, the com-parison shows that gross rent is more volatile than assessed value.

The evidence leaves no doubt that a gross-rent tax base is

[25] *Experience in Urban Real Estate Investment* (New York, Columbia Univer-sity Press, 1955).
[26] See Appendix B, Table B.2.

unstable over severe cycles such as the Great Depression (or the long building cycle that spanned the interwar period). Yet one may question the relevance of that kind of experience for current policy. Gross rent is not unstable over the course of the minor cycles such as we have had since 1945. If one is convinced that both the business cycle and the building cycle have been "tamed," then he ought not to object to a gross-rent tax base on grounds of instability.

Next consider the stability of tax No. 4, a real estate net-income tax. To estimate the cyclical movement of this tax base, we have two sets of data.[27] The first is a Commerce Department series on the net income, before taxes, of rental and owner-occupied housing. Comparisons between the Commerce Department net-income data and the New York City assessment series are subject to the same limitation described above in connection with gross rent. Therefore, we shall again restrict the discussion to the period of the Great Depression: net rental from all housing declined 55 percent from 1929 to its depression low point in 1934. This was more than three times the percentage decline in New York City assessed valuations to their 1935 low and more than two and one-half times the decline to their 1944–45 low point. (See Table 10.5.) It compares with a decline of only 36 percent in Commerce Department gross rents over the same years.

The second comparison between tax No. 4 and tax No. 2 makes use of data derived from Grebler's study of selected New York City properties. The derived series shows the movement of net income before taxes or depreciation for the sample properties for five-year periods down to 1945–49 and for the terminal year, 1950. From its 1925–29 peak, this series fell about 47 percent to 1935–39 and about 49 percent to 1940–44, after which it began to rise once more. (See Table 10.5.) Since the five-year averages damp the peak-to-trough movement, it is safe to say that a yearly series would show a drop of well above 50 percent. Moreover, deduction of the relatively stable charges for depreciation and debt would undoubtedly leave an

27 See Appendix B, Table B.3.

even less stable net-income residual. After due allowance for error, it remains clear that these data confirm the instability of net income as a tax base when compared with assessed valuation.

Indeed, real estate net income was so volatile over the course of the 1929–37 business cycle that one might imagine there were years in the early 1930s in which real estate taxes paid exceeded the whole net amount. Such is not the case, however: the Commerce Department data show that total net rent after real estate taxes was never negative, although net after tax rents fell almost to zero on rented farm property in 1932 and on rented housing in 1934 and 1935.

When net rents on the aggregate of rental housing fell disastrously during the Great Depression, it is certain that a good many properties were showing losses. Thus, as Rapkin has pointed out, the burden of a net-income tax would shift to a smaller number of properties during a depression.[28] But, as in the case of a gross-rent tax, arguments from depression experience are not conclusive: one may believe that major cycles will not recur, and there is no evidence that net income is unstable over minor cycles.

Tax No. 5, the British "rates," is based on assessed gross rent modified by a deduction for expenses. It would be pointless to attempt a statistical comparison of the stability of the British base with that of tax No. 2 by the technique we have used in this chapter, since the taxes were applied in differently fluctuating economies. One would have to use an elasticity measure which is far more complex than anything we can attempt here. Even that would not take into account institutional differences between the two economies.

If tax No. 5 were applied in the United States, one would expect its base to be somewhat less stable cyclically than that of the traditional American tax. Assume that assessments for both taxes are kept up to date and fully reflect changes in the market. Then tax No. 5 would tend to be less stable because

[28] Chester Rapkin, "Role of Real Estate Taxes in the Investment Experience of Real Property," *Appraisal Journal*, October, 1954, p. 496.

the current gross earning power of a property may well fluctuate more than its capital value over the cycle, since the latter is related to all expected future returns, the good years taken with the bad, while the former reflects only the current market.

If, as we assumed, assessments fully reflected the current market, one would expect the base of tax No. 5 to be just as variable over the cycle as that of tax No. 3, based on actual gross rent. Indeed, the former might be *more* variable, since long-term leases impart a degree of stability to the latter. But if assessment practice resembled that which actually exists for tax No. 2 in the United States in not fully reflecting market cycles, then it seems likely that the base of tax No. 5 would be less rather than more unstable than that of tax No. 3. We are probably safe in concluding that in practice tax No. 5 would be more stable than tax No. 3 and less stable than tax No. 2.

The stability of tax No. 6, an abatement, and tax No. 7, a penalty, would depend on that of the basic tax with which they were combined.

Revenue Criteria—Adequacy of Yield

Local governments may envy Washington its ability to cut tax rates, reform tax law at the expense of the revenue, and even abandon a number of levies outright from time to time, but so great are the pressures for local expenditure that they are not now in a position to imitate its example. It is quite clear, therefore, that any proposal for real estate tax reform must, if it is to be taken seriously at this date, pass the test of adequacy of yield. With such considerations in mind, it would appear sensible to take the yield of the present American tax, with rates now in force, as a standard of adequacy. We will then ask whether the base of each proposed alternative tax could possibly yield as much as the present levy.

In discussing adequacy of yield, we have to deal with two variables: the size of the base and the level of the rate. Some curious results are possible in extreme cases. For instance, some kinds of taxes could be levied at rates above 100 percent, others not. A tax on assessed capital value such as tax No. 2 can be levied at rates above 100 percent without absorbing the whole value or net rent of real estate. In fact, such a tax would not absorb the whole net rent until the rate rose to infinity, for the capital value (which is the tax base) recedes, on account of tax capitalization, as the rate rises. On the other hand, a tax on the gross rent of real estate could not be raised to 100 percent. If set permanently at 100 percent, it would obviously make private ownership impossible. If raised to 100 percent even temporarily, it would cause private owners to shut down. Nevertheless, a gross-rent tax could be raised to a very high rate without inevitably breaking down, since at least some landlords could raise rents high enough to cover the tax and still pay their expenses.

A tax on net rent or net income raises different problems. Paradoxically, the tax collector can, over short periods, absorb more than the pre-tax net rent of real estate and get away with it, provided that the tax base is something other than net rent. Indeed, such occurrences are not uncommon: on particular properties, especially in hard times, it must often happen that tax No. 2 absorbs more than the pre-tax net income; such is inevitably the case for vacant properties. Yet it is equally clear that if net income is the tax base, then the tax rate cannot reach 100 percent consistent with private ownership. A rate set permanently at 100 percent would obviously put an end to private ownership by confiscating the whole return. But neither would a temporary rate of 100 percent be feasible. Owners would certainly find ways to reduce or to avoid showing net income in years when the tax rate even approached 100 percent. Local tax collectors lack the facilities to enforce honest compliance under such circumstances.

Bearing these extreme possibilities in mind, we can now examine the adequacy of the alternative tax bases. There can be no question about the adequacy of the gross-rent base of tax No. 3. Whatever sums have been successfully extracted by means of tax No. 2 either recently or during the Depression were, in fact, paid out of gross rent. The principal difference when the tax is based on gross rent rather than value is that in the former case landlords are encouraged to shut down to avoid taxes when their gross rent no longer covers operating expenses plus taxes, whereas in the latter they shut down only when rents fail to cover operating expenses alone. Thus, during a depression, a gross-rent tax would encourage boarding up. This would not necessarily diminish the gross-rent base, however, since displaced tenants would move into the remaining buildings, where gross rent would consequently rise.

The same logic applies in the case of tax No. 5, the British "rates." In this case the tax base is smaller than total gross rent by the amount of the allowable deductions for expenses. But since the deductions are calculated as a percentage of the gross rent, they can never result in the tax base falling to zero, as, conceivably, it might in the case of a true net-rent tax. The base of tax No. 5 must be pronounced adequate on the same grounds as that of tax No. 3.

Tax No. 1, on the assessed value of land, almost certainly fails to pass the test of adequacy of yield. It is common knowledge that Henry George's single-tax proposal has been defeated not only by its opponents but also by the march of history, since the sum of all public expenditures in the United States has long since out-distanced the whole rent of land. Less widely known is the fact that the yield of the American real estate tax itself is now catching up with or perhaps has already passed the sum of all that economic surplus. Unless we are prepared virtually to end private ownership of rights in land by taking almost its whole rent, it is no longer feasible to substitute a land tax for the real estate tax at the present level of yield. Since it is safe to say that the American public is not prepared to go that far in land taxation, tax No. 1 fails to pass the test of adequacy.

Before examining the relevant data, it is worth while posing the question mathematically. We wish to discover under what conditions it will necessarily follow that the rent of land will exceed the desired yield of the tax. Let

N_L = rent of land gross of real estate tax on land

R = yield of present American real estate tax

t = rate of present tax on assessed value of land and buildings

C_L = capital value of land after capitalization of present land tax

= assessed value of land

C_B – capital value of buildings after capitalization or shifting of present building tax

= assessed value of buildings

i = rate of interest for capitalization of rent of land

It can then be shown that

$$N_L > R$$

is possible if and only if [29]

$$i/t > C_B/C_L$$

We can investigate the likelihood that the above condition will be fulfilled by examining, first, data for the United States as a whole, and, second, data for the interesting case of New York City. (Details about the derivation of statistics used in the following section will be found in Appendix C.)

For the United States as a whole, we can calculate the

[29] The proposition can be demonstrated as follows:

$$N_L = C_L(i + t)$$
$$R = t(C_L + C_B)$$

Therefore,

$$N_L > R$$

can be written as

$$C_L(i + t) > t(C_L + C_B)$$

or as

$$iC_L + tC_L > tC_L + tC_B$$

which reduces to

$$iC_L > tC_B$$

or, by rearrangement of terms, to

$$i/t > C_B/C_L$$

It has been pointed out that computing the rent of land, N_L, by multiplication of the capital value of land by some normal rate of return will give an estimate of current rent that is too high if current land values are being drawn upward by an expectation that land rent as a whole will rise in the future. There is, however, no way of measuring the size of the error thus introduced into N_L as we calculate it. This point is raised in Joseph S. Keiper, Ernest Kurnow, Clifford D. Clark, and Harvey H. Segal, *Theory and Measurement of Rent* (Philadelphia, Chilton, 1961), p. 99.

ratio of the value of buildings to the value of land from data published by Raymond Goldsmith.[30] His data indicate that in the United States in 1956 the ratio of taxable buildings to taxable land was about 2.9:1. It is desirable, however, to exclude farm land and buildings in order to obtain a figure more nearly representative of urban areas. That done, the ratio of the value of private, noninstitutional, nonfarm buildings to the value of land works out to be 4.4:1 in 1956. These results are, to be sure, highly approximate.[31]

Next, using both the Goldsmith data and figures from the Census Bureau for 1956 and 1957, we can estimate the national average effective rate of the real estate tax, i.e., the ratio of tax revenue to the full market value of property. These calculations indicate a tax rate, t, of about 1.5 percent.

To complete our calculation, it remains only to estimate i, the average rate of interest for capitalization of the rent of land. Since land is commonly regarded as a secure asset for long-term investment purposes, the capitalization rate is apparently rather low, probably in the range of 5 or 6 percent.[32] We shall use the 6 percent rate in the calculations that follow in order not to underestimate the probable rent of land.

The algebraic test now gives the following result: In 1956 the ratio of i to t was approximately 0.06 to 0.015, or 4:1; in the same year the ratio of all taxable building values to all taxable land values was approximately 2.9:1. Therefore, the rent of land was still somewhat in excess of the total yield of the real estate tax. If, however, we eliminate the farm sector, we get the opposite result: the ratio of nonfarm buildings to land was approximately 4.4:1; therefore, the rent of all nonfarm land fell slightly short of the yield of the real estate tax on

30 *The National Wealth of the United States in the Postwar Period* (Princeton, N.J., Princeton University Press, 1962). See also Appendix C, Table C.1, of this book.

31 See note 1 of Appendix C.

32 Robert M. Haig calculated the probable effect on land value of an increase in the land tax on alternative assumptions of a 5 percent and a 6 percent capitalization rate. *Some Probable Effects of the Exemption of Improvements from Taxation in the City of New York,* a report prepared for the Committee on Taxation in the City of New York (New York, 1915), p. 131.

nonfarm land and buildings combined. (For lack of data we must assume that t is the same for the nonfarm sector as for all taxable property.) Thus, for the nation as a whole, excluding the farm sector, tax No. 1 on site value cannot provide adequate revenue according to this test.[33] Of course, this fact does not logically preclude the possibility that in some localities land values are high enough and the present level of real estate tax rates low enough to make the tax arithmetically (if not politically) feasible.

Such, however, is apparently not the case in the one city where we have made the test. New York City annually assesses land and buildings separately, thus providing another (and independent) set of useful data.[34] In 1960–61 the ratio of the assessed value of taxable buildings to taxable land was 1.94:1— a much lower ratio of buildings to land than for nonfarm areas as a whole. Nevertheless, the tax rate of 0.0424 was so high that the total real estate tax bill appears to have exceeded the whole rent of land, for the ratio of i (estimated at 0.06) to l was only 1.41:1.

The above test assumes that New York City's real estate is assessed at its full value. In fact, assessment tends to lag behind market value when the latter is rising, as it has been since World War II. We estimate that by 1960–61 the ratio of New York City assessments to market value may have fallen to about 75 percent. In that case, our algebraic test is appropriately adjusted by lowering the effective tax rate 25 percent from 0.0424 to 0.0318. Even then, however, the rent of land remains below the total real estate tax bill—for the ratio of

---

[33] Keiper et al. *(Theory and Measurement of Rent,* Chap. 7) provide an independent estimate of land rent against which to check conclusions reached using Goldsmith's data. The Keiper estimate of total real property value in 1956 is very close to Goldsmith's, but the share of land is somewhat higher and of improvements somewhat lower than in Goldsmith's study. Differences in approach and the lack of detail in the Keiper data make exact comparisons difficult, but it is probable that using their data with the methods employed here the rent of land would be well in excess of the yield of the present American real estate tax. Even for the nonfarm sector, land rent would probably somewhat exceed the necessary tax revenue.

[34] See Appendix C, Table C.2.

i to *t* rises from 1.41:1 to 1.88:1 but remains below the building-to-land ratio of 1.94:1.

Fifty years ago the same test in New York City would have yielded the opposite result. When a bill was introduced in the New York State legislature in 1915 which would have allowed New York City to shift the whole burden of the real estate tax from land and improvements to land alone, the proposition was far from being an arithmetical absurdity, both because the real estate tax rate was then much lower and the ratio of land value to improvement value was then much higher.[35]

The estimates presented above are, indeed, subject to an important qualification. Strictly speaking they may be valid only in the very short run, since they make use of a measure of land rent derived from the estimated *current* capital value of land. Now, the current capital value of land reflects the influence of the present tax on improvements. As pointed out in Chapter 3, it is possible, though not certain a priori, that a tax on improvements reduces site rent by depressing the demand for sites. In that case, untaxing improvements would eventually cause land rent to increase, and the maximum possible yield of a tax on site value accompanied by the untaxing of improvements might be greater in the long run than the estimates above suggest.

It would, however, be imprudent, to say the least, for any local government to bank on such an effect. At most, the argument would seem to suggest the economic feasibility of a gradual reduction of the building tax accompanied by a gradual increase in the tax rate on land. Such a plan, if carried out over a long enough period, would enable a locality to observe the effects on land rent of untaxing buildings and to adjust its tax program accordingly. Such flexibility is, however, likely to be politically unattainable: tax laws are changed only infrequently and with great effort, and basic matters such as the ratio of land taxes to building taxes are not left open to be contested in recurring battle. The Pittsburgh "graded tax plan," described in Chapter 9 and discussed again in the concluding

[35] Haig, *Some Probable Effects, passim.*

section of this chapter, was not flexible in this sense. It provided for gradual reduction of the ratio of the building rate to the land rate but on a prearranged schedule with the fixed goal of ultimately achieving a 1:2 ratio.

Next, consider a net-income tax on real estate. The adequacy of the base of tax No. 4 varies over the business cycle. In properous times or in years of moderate recessions, such as those that have occurred since 1945, the tax base is undoubtedly large enough to yield the necessary revenues. We lack data on more recent cycles, but the recession of 1949 does not show up at all in the aggregate net-rent figures of the Commerce Department series referred to above. Indeed, this is hardly surprising in view of the prevalence of comparatively long-term rent contracts. As H. D. Osborne put it in describing the Commerce Department data, net rents "have been comparatively little affected by short-period fluctuations, and consequently have risen as a percentage of national income in such years as 1938, 1946, and 1949." [36]

In a major depression, however, a net-rent base might prove inadequate, not because aggregate net rents would fall below the level of required taxes (we have already shown that they did not do so even in the worst years of the Great Depression) but because so many properties would show losses that the rate on the remaining profitable ones would have to rise to prohibitive levels. Even if this were politically feasible, it would not be administratively so, as we have already pointed out.

The issue turns, then, on how certain one is that major depressions will henceforth be avoided. Perhaps the most prudent answer is that the adequacy of yield of tax No. 4 is "uncertain."

The adequacy of yield of tax No. 6, an abatement, and tax No. 7, a penalty, would depend, first of all, on the basic tax with which they were combined. In addition, tax No. 6 would at first be likely to reduce revenues below what they would have been in the absence of an abatement, for some

36 *Survey of Current Business,* June, 1953, p. 17.

projects that would have gone ahead even without an abatement are likely to benefit from the relief. If, however, the abatement is temporary, it might lead eventually to greater revenues than would otherwise have occurred. The effect of tax No. 6 on yield is therefore uncertain.

The effect of tax No. 7 on the yield of the basic tax with which it is combined was discussed in detail in Chapters 7 and 8. It is likely (but not certain) that tax No. 7 would increase tax revenues but probably by no more than an insignificant percentage.

Our conclusions on stability and adequacy of yield are summarized in Table 10.6.

TABLE 10.6

Stability and Adequacy of Yield

Tax Type	Stability as Compared with Tax No. 2	Adequacy as Compared with Tax No. 2
No. 1 (capital value of site)	Uncertain	Probably inadequate
No. 3 (gross rent)	Somewhat less stable	Adequate
No. 4 (net income)	Much less stable	Adequate barring severe depression
No. 5 (British "rates")	Depends upon assessment practice	Adequate
No. 6 (abatement)	...	...
No. 7 (penalty)	...	...

Equity Arguments for Property Taxation

Our final criterion of choice is equity: certainly important, fundamentally subjective, eternally argued over. Our treatment is based on the proposition that at this date in the history of our economic development the old contention that real estate taxes, as a general class, are "equitable" does not stand up. Specifically, we agree with many other modern tax analysts that neither the "ability to pay" nor the "benefit" criterion of equity can justify the use of a real estate tax at the current level of yield. If we thought that any of the proposed alternative taxes could be justified on either of these grounds, we would wish to apply these criteria uniformly to all the others. To the contrary, however, we believe that under modern (and especially modern urban) conditions, neither is applicable.

Economists who have analyzed the real estate tax generally agree that ability-to-pay arguments (however one chooses to define ability to pay) do not support it.[37] Before the Industrial Revolution, when personal wealth was accumulated mostly in the form of real property, a tax on real property may have been the best available way of taxing roughly in accordance with ability to pay. However that may be, the tax can no longer be justified on ability-to-pay grounds. Today we can measure income accurately; and personal income, not the extent of one's use of real property or ownership of land, is the appropriate measure of ability to pay.

Whether or not the tax is regressive to income is a different question. On the basis of studies indicating that the income elasticity of demand for housing was less than unity, it was once widely agreed to by economists that the tax was regressive. Recent studies by Margaret Reid and Richard Muth [38] indicate an income elasticity above unity and therefore a progressive tax. But one cannot call the tax equitable simply because its burden correlates with income in the way one favors. To do that is to adopt as a standard what William S. Vickrey has called "statistical equity," treating the statistical average man but not any particular man equitably.

The notion that real estate taxes are justified because they are in proportion to benefits conferred on property owners or tenants is plausible up to a point. The benefit argument fails, however, because the yield of the tax far exceeds the cost of those local expenditures which confer benefits on owners of real property or their tenants in amounts that may reasonably

[37] See, for example: John Due, *Government Finance* (Homewood, Ill., Richard D. Irwin, 1954), pp. 402–3; Clarence Heer, "The Property Tax as a Measure of Ability," in *Property Taxes*, pp. 155–64; Shultz and Harriss, *American Public Finance*, pp. 402–3.

[38] Margaret Reid, *Housing and Income* (Chicago, University of Chicago Press, 1962), pp. 376–78; Richard Muth, "The Demand for Non-Farm Housing," in Arnold C. Harberger, ed., *The Demand for Durable Goods* (Chicago, University of Chicago Press, 1960).

be related to the assessed value, gross rent, net income, or other tax basis of the property itself. Since we take the present yield of the tax as a datum, we must therefore reject the benefit justification—a statement which we can support with reasonably accurate data once we have clarified the meaning of "benefit."

Since urban life without urban government is scarcely possible and since urban property (improvements as well as land) would be worth little or nothing without the dense settlements which we understand by "urban life," it can be argued that almost every kind of local expenditure enhances urban property values and in that sense confers a "benefit" on property owners. Taxes to pay for such expenditures could then be called "benefit" taxes. But unless the benefit received is in proportion to and worth at least as much as the tax paid, it is misleading to call the levy a benefit tax. To the extent that a given levy is a benefit tax, if both the tax and the services it pays for are canceled, those who are relieved of both will seek to provide the same service for themselves privately. If they wish to provide the service privately but in amounts which individually bear little relation to the tax formerly paid, then the tax, even though it financed a beneficial service, was not, properly speaking, a benefit tax.

Consider two examples: refuse collection and public school education. If refuse is not collected by the municipality, owners or tenants will have to arrange for its removal privately. Refuse production in a residential building is probably a function of the number of occupants and of their general level of consumption. On both counts it would be positively related to the assessed value of the building: the larger the number of tenants in a building and the higher the rent (and hence consumption) level of the occupants, the higher the assessed value would generally be, other things equal. Hence, tax No. 2 on the assessed value of real property, if used to pay for refuse collection, might be classified (very roughly, to be sure) as a benefit tax.

Education, however, is a far different case. Although all families benefit from the externalities of education, only a fraction of them receive the direct benefit of having their own children's schooling paid for. The relationship between property values and the demand for public school education is not close enough in most localities to enable one to classify a property tax that pays for schools as a benefit tax.

Indeed, it is difficult to draw a clear line between those municipal services whose benefits are closely related to property values (or other property bases) and those whose benefits are not. For example, it is sometimes argued that fire protection confers a benefit on property owners in proportion to property value, and that therefore this much of local expenditure can justifiably be paid for by tax No. 2. This is one of the strongest cases among those that support the benefit argument. Yet even this case is flawed. For example, personal property receives as much protection as real property but usually pays little or no tax. Or, as William S. Vickrey has pointed out, "replacing an old, obsolescent building with a modern fireproof one may lessen the amount of benefit obtained from fire protection even though the value of the property be increased." [39]

It is also argued that police protection confers benefits in proportion to property value. This is a weak case, however, except in so far as the police suppress vandalism and arson, because real property is clearly not subject to theft. In any event, a large fraction of police effort is devoted to traffic control, protection against riot and assault, suppression of vice, etc., the benefits from which can be related only very tenuously to ownership or tenure of real property. At best then, a small proportion of the cost of police protection is chargeable to real property on a benefit basis.

If, however, we wish to measure the validity of the benefit argument statistically, we must draw the line somewhere. Let us measure benefit, as above, by the value of direct services rendered to property owners or tenants as such. In that case the following services of local governments may be thought of

[39] "General and Specific Financing of Urban Services," in Howard G. Schaller, ed., *Public Expenditure Decisions in the Urban Community* (Washington, D.C., Resources for the Future, Inc., 1963), p. 64.

as beneficial: sanitation, sewers and sewage disposal, highways (i.e., streets), water supply, fire protection, and police protection. In order to make the strongest possible case for the property tax as a benefit levy, we shall assign the whole cost of each of these services as a benefit to property, with the exception of police protection, of which we count only one-third as a property benefit.

TABLE 10.7

Estimated Value of Local Services Chargeable to Property Users, U.S. Totals 1960

Local Service	Local Expenditure (Less User Charges, etc.) ($ millions)
Sanitation	624
Sewers and sewage disposal ᵃ	681
Highways ᵇ	1,925
Water supply ᶜ	352
Fire protection	995
Police protection (33% of $1,612 million)	537
Total of above services	5,114
Less: special assessments for public improvements	369
Equals: balance chargeable to property tax	4,745
Property tax revenue	15,798
Ratio of Balance to Property tax revenue	0.303

ᵃ Expenditures for sewers and sewage disposal less current revenues from sewers and other sanitation.

ᵇ Local expenditure for highways less local user charges and state aid for local highways.

ᶜ Operating and capital expenditures less system revenues.

Source: U.S. Department of Commerce, Bureau of the Census, *Governmental Finances in 1960,* Tables 1, 3, 4, and 7.

A part of the cost of the above services is paid for by user charges, special assessments, or state aid. That part must be deducted from the total to arrive at a sum which localities could legitimately cover by a property tax as a benefit levy. Calculations based on Census Bureau data for 1960 are presented in Table 10.7. In that year local property tax revenues amounted to $15.8 billion. Expenditures directly beneficial to property users less costs met by user charges, special assessments, and state aid, totaled $4.7 billion. Thus, only 30 percent of property tax revenue was required to cover the cost of services directly beneficial to property, even when benefits are estimated very liberally. The ratio would be slightly higher if revenue from personal property were deducted from total property tax revenue. We conclude that a property tax on the scale of the present American levy cannot possibly be justified by the benefit argument.,

Nevertheless, the question remains: given that we must have a real estate tax in one form or another, which alternative is most equitable? We shall deal with tax No. 1 at length below. Let us here consider the other basic types, each on its own merits, that is, setting aside the inequities that may arise if we switch from one to another.

Tax No. 4 on real estate net income relies for its justification in equity on the ability-to-pay argument. But we have rejected the use of that argument on the grounds that ability to pay must refer to persons, whereas the real estate tax takes property as its base. Tax No. 4 is therefore simply a tax on profits earned in a particular set of businesses.

The remaining alternatives (again leaving out tax No. 1 for the moment) have relied principally on the benefit argument for justification, but we have rejected that, too. If these alternatives are not user charges, what are they? Taxes No. 3 and No. 5, the gross rent tax and the British "rates," can be thought of as variations of the excise tax, applied to the consumption of real estate services, for in the long run that portion of the tax that is paid on improvements is passed on to the consumer. Both of these are true consumption taxes, since they apply only when services are actually consumed—vacant properties are exempt. Tax No. 2, the traditional American levy, is, strictly speaking, a wealth rather than a consumption tax. It applies to wealth held in a certain form regardless of whether it is used or yields current income. The portion of the tax levied on improvements tends, however, in the long run to be borne by the wealth-user rather than the wealth-owner, so it closely resembles a tax on the consumption of real estate services.

As between a profits tax, a wealth tax, or a consumption tax applied to only one class of business, there is little ground for preference on considerations of equity. We therefore rank taxes Nos. 2, 3, 4, and 5 as equally equitable.

Equity Aspects of Tax No. 1

The site value or unimproved value of land is an economic surplus which has long attracted economists as a particularly fit object for taxation.[40] If the state had always taken, say, 80 percent of land rent in taxes, there would be no grounds for objecting to such a tax as inequitable. But in the case of tax No. 1, one cannot overlook the inequities that would arise in shifting a given tax load from a broad base, such as gross rent or value of land and improvements combined, to the much narrower base of site value only. Shifting to tax No. 1 today would take for the state much if not all of the value of land, which is to treat landowners inequitably as compared with owners of wealth in other forms, for, however unearned past increments in land value may have been when they occurred, present owners may have paid anything up to full value for their investments; it will not do to expropriate them on the ground that past owners at various times received unearned increments. This is an old but very weighty argument against resort to heavier land taxation. In answer to it, one might point out that the proposition is not just to tax land more but to remove the tax on buildings and put it on land. This has two possible consequences: First, the relief to buildings might help landowners indirectly if the resulting long-run increase in the

40 To quote some of those who cannot be labeled single-taxers, Pigou wrote: "The unimproved or public value of land is, economically speaking, an exceptionally good object for taxation." *Land Taxation*, p. 32. Seligman put it thus: "While I hold the arguments of the single taxers to be erroneous, I agree with the majority of the modern economists in the belief that land values afford an especially promising and suitable basis for local taxation." Edwin R. A. Seligman, *Studies in Public Finance* (New York, Macmillan, 1925), p. 272.

stock of shelter causes land rent, gross of tax, to rise. Second, the relief afforded on buildings might compensate landowners directly for the extra burden on land.

Regarding the first point, it is quite certain that untaxing buildings would increase the equilibrium stock of shelter, but it is less certain what or how much effect this would have on the level of land rent. To the extent that land rent, gross of tax, rose, landowners would receive an offset to their increased tax burden. But the extent of the possible offset is not something that can be determined by a priori analysis, since, as pointed out in Chapter 3, it depends on both the elasticity of demand for shelter and the relationship between demand schedules for shelter on different sites, and these matters can be determined only empirically. Nor is it possible to say that there is likely to be at least a small offset and therefore that one could without inequity transfer at least a small part of the present building tax onto land, for the extent of the offset, if any, is likely to depend upon the extent of the tax change—the less buildings are freed of burden, the smaller the possible rise in land rent gross of tax. Unless it can be shown that a substantial compensating rise in land rent is highly probable, the argument that it would be inequitable to landowners to load the whole real estate tax onto the site-value base will continue to be persuasive.

Turning to the second point, to what extent does the tax relief on their buildings directly compensate owners of parcels of real property for the extra tax burden on their land? We will examine the problem under alternative assumptions. These are (1) that on every parcel of land there is an improvement and that the ratio of improvement value to land value is everywhere the same; (non-1) a situation in which (1) does *not* hold; (2) that new construction is possible at all levels of rent if improvements are untaxed; and (non-2) that (2) does not hold. We assume throughout that land and improvement are invariably owned in common. To simplify the argument, we also assume that land rent gross of tax does not rise as a consequence of the tax relief to buildings.

Consider first the problem of equity among owners of rental properties if buildings are untaxed and the revenue lost thereby is regained by raising the land tax. (This is precisely what would occur upon the adoption of tax No. 1 in our analytical framework.) If condition (1) obtained, all property owners would be treated alike. Each would find his tax bill at first unchanged. He would now pay on land the same amount of tax he formerly paid on land and improvements. If condition (non-1) obtained—which is, in fact, the case—those owners whose ratio of building value to land value was below the aggregate ratio would find their immediate tax bill raised; those whose ratio of building value to land value was above the aggregate ratio would find it reduced. Thus far the argument is an old and familiar one.

In order to discuss effects beyond the immediate period of the tax change, we must introduce assumptions as to new construction. If we assume (2) obtains in conjunction either with (1) or (non-1), then as new construction occurs, rents will gradually decline at all rent levels. New construction attributable to the untaxing of buildings will continue until rents have fallen by the amount of the forgiven building tax. When that point is reached, owners of old buildings will have lost the offset they originally enjoyed to their heavier land tax. Landowners, therefore, are not permanently compensated for the heavier land tax by untaxing buildings. They are compensated only during the initial period before the untaxing of buildings relieves building rent. Under the assumption (non-1), however, it is possible that owners of very valuable buildings on relatively cheap land would gain enough in the initial period to offset or more than offset even the permanent confiscation of their land rent. At the opposite pole, owners of vacant land obviously receive no offset, even temporarily.

If, on the other hand, we assume (non-2) to obtain either in conjunction with (1) or (non-1), then the effects are still more diverse. If, as is likely to be the case, the untaxing of buildings makes new construction more profitable at the upper rental levels and opens up additional middle-rent levels to new building but does not make new construction feasible for the lower rent brackets, then owners of old buildings at low rent levels will retain the benefit derived from untaxing buildings much longer than owners of old middle- and upper- bracket buildings. In the long run, however, it seems likely that rents would decline even in the lower rent brackets as a result of the pressure of new construction and lower rents in the levels above.

This analysis also helps to answer the question of equity as among tenants. If (2) obtains, tenants at all rental levels will benefit by a uniform proportionate reduction in rents. If (non-2) holds, tenants in the middle and upper rental brackets will benefit sooner than those in the lower (or slum) category. How long it would take the benefits of untaxing buildings to "filter down" to the lowest level under assumption (non-2), it is impossible to say.

What about equity as among owner-occupants and as between owner-occupants and landlords or tenants? As among owner-occupants, if (1) obtains, then all are treated alike and find their tax bill unchanged. If (non-1) holds, the individual tax burdens change in the same manner as among owners of rental buildings.

The immediate effect of the shift to tax No. 1 would be to depress land values by the capitalized amount of the added tax. On the other hand, values of existing buildings would at first rise, though not necessarily by the same amount. Assuming that (2) obtains, new construction of units for owner-occupancy would soon begin to cut back the initial rise in building values at all levels of value. Building values would continue to decline under the influence of the new construction induced by untaxing until they reached the level of cost of replacement from which their initial rise began. If (1) obtains—together with (2)—owner-occupants would continue to pay the same amount of tax they paid before the shift to tax No. 1. But if they sold their property, they would now receive less for it—its land value would have declined while its building value would be unchanged. If they did not sell their property, the same effect would show up in the fact that imputed rent value of the space they own would have declined; or to look at it another way, if they now chose to rent their house to someone else, they would receive less rent than before for house and land combined. Rents would have declined because of the increased supply of shelter space. Thus, if both (1) and (2) obtained, owner-occupants, as owners, would receive the same treatment as would owners of rental property: their permanent loss on land would not be compensated by the temporary gain on buildings. If (non-2) and/or (non-1) obtained, their experience would again parallel that of owner-renters and need not be recapitulated here.

In their role as tenants, owner-occupants would eventually receive the same benefit as tenants of rental property. This would show up in the fact that, as noted above, the imputed rental paid by the owner-occupant (as tenant) would decline, once again with modifications according as (1) or (non-1) and (2) or (non-2) obtained.

How would owner-occupants' gains as tenants compare with their losses as owners? If (1) and (2) obtained, each would gain as a tenant just enough to offset his loss as an owner of land. But if (non-1) and/or (non-2) obtained, gains and losses would not necessarily be evenly distributed. For example, if (non-1) and (2) obtained, the owner of a relatively valuable house on relatively worthless land would find his tax bill reduced. His loss as an owner would be relatively slight, since he would have little land value to lose. His gain as a tenant would be relatively large, since building rents would eventually decline by the amount of the forgiven building tax, which in this case would be relatively large. His gain as tenant would outweigh his loss as owner: such an owner-occupant would make a net gain if tax No. 1 were adopted.

Since conditions (non-1) and (non-2) appear to rule in the housing market, it is clear not only that the treatment of owner-occupants will vary case by case but also that owner-occupants in the aggregate might gain or lose at the expense of other classes in the aggregate if tax No. 1 were adopted.

More generally, it follows that the benefits or the burdens accruing from a switch to tax No. 1 might, for a long time at any rate, flow toward one income class more than another.

Equity Aspects of Taxes No. 6 and No. 7

Much the same kind of analysis as was developed above for tax No. 1 can be made of tax No. 6, a tax abatement. For convenience, let us assume that tax No. 6 is used in conjunction with the traditional American tax No. 2. Thus far we have considered tax No. 6 mainly in its application to maintenance and rehabilitation. In these cases the authorities would agree not to raise the tax base of the property (at least for a given term) if the owner undertook either operating or capital improvements. The principle can, however, readily be extended to take in new construction: the owner would be permitted to build a new structure while paying taxes (at least for a given term) only on the value of the previously existing improvements.

Now, in any of these forms an abatement involves unequal treatment of owners of properties of equal value. Does this make for serious inequity? Helped by an abatement, new build ers, new rehabilitators, and owners improving their standard of operation would gain an advantage over other owners. On similar properties they would obtain a higher net return at the same rents.

The abatement would continue to stimulate investment until the stock of housing had been enlarged or rehabilitated to the point where the return on further such investment fell to the level obtainable by using capital in other ways. It would stimulate improved quality of operation in certain units in the manner already described in Chapter 7. The combined effect of an enlarged and rehabilitated stock of housing and improved quality of operation in select buildings would be to reduce rents in the aggregate of nonqualifying structures below the level that prevailed before abatements began. In other words, the prospective return on marginal new investments or operating improvements which benefit from abatement would be controlling. The result would be plainly inequitable to all those owners of previously constructed buildings who were not in a position to take advantage of abatements.

A second round of loss would occur to nonqualifying owners if revenue needs were such that the abatement to some improvements meant that a higher tax rate would have to be applied to remaining taxpaying properties. This would obviously be the case if, as is probable, some of the improvements that benefit by tax abatement would have been undertaken even without such aid. But it remains a legitimate complaint even if none of them would have been undertaken in the absence of the abatement, since the abated improvements might well drive some formerly taxpaying properties out of business or at least reduce their taxability. In short, a tax abatement such as tax No. 6 discriminates among property owners.

Next, consider the effects of tax No. 6 upon equitable treatment of tenants. In so far as the tax encourages improved quality of operation, its effects are deliberately restricted to buildings in the slum category, which means that it benefits mainly the lower income groups. In so far as the tax encourages new construction or rehabilitation, its effect on tenants depends upon whether condition (2) or (non-2) obtains. If (2) obtains, the tax would encourage investment in housing at all rent levels and would therefore bring about a uniform reduction of rents for all rent (and hence income) classes. If (non-2) obtains, the early benefit of new construction and rehabilitation accrues only to the higher rent (and income) classes. Lower rents would spread downward into the low-rent (and income) sectors only very gradually.

Tax No. 7, a penalty against substandard buildings, raises rather different problems, as suggested above in the discussion of administrative feasibility. The appropriate question is not whether tax No. 7 is equitable by comparison with other taxes but whether it is equitable by comparison with building codes, a matter we do not propose to deal with in this study.

Summary of Findings

We have now measured the alternative taxes against all ten criteria of choice. What are the most telling points that have been made for and against each tax? What conclusions do they lead to?

Tax No. 1, the site-value levy, is neutral to operating, rate of replacement of structure, remodeling, and new construction decisions—four strong arguments in its favor. If levied on capital value, it is neutral to land-use decisions. It is neutral with respect to the use or nonuse of existing housing and neutral as between owner-occupied and rental housing. It would be somewhat more difficult to administer than tax No. 2, the tax on combined value of land and improvements. Changing from tax No. 2 to tax No. 1 would help tenants in the aggregate at the expense of landowners in the aggregate. The two most serious arguments against such a change are inadequacy of yield and inequitable treatment of landowners. These are sufficiently important to make site value unacceptable as the sole basis of the contemporary real estate tax, but they do not rule out a compromise involving use of a relatively heavier land tax.

Tax No. 2, the present American levy, does not have harmful effects on quality of operation or condition of structure. It is certainly a deterrent to remodeling or new construction, and this is its greatest defect. It is neutral with respect to land-use decisions and decisions with respect to the use or nonuse of existing housing. In principle, if not in practice, it is neutral as between rental and owner-occupied housing. It is relatively easy to administer and provides adequate revenue (this last by definition). Its revenue yield is relatively stable. It is neither more nor less equitable than taxes Nos. 3, 4, and 5.

Tax No. 3, on gross rent, has negative effects on quality of operation and condition of structure and is also a deterrent to remodeling and new construction—four serious defects. It is not neutral among land uses, since it favors both noncommercial and deferred uses. It encourages boarding up of rental housing during a depression. Special provisions would be needed to make the tax applicable to owner-occupied properties. On grounds of administrative feasibility, it ranks about the same as the present American tax. The tax yield would be adequate but somewhat less stable than that of tax No. 2. It raises no special problems of equity. Compared with the present American real estate tax, tax No. 3 has no advantages and numerous drawbacks.

Tax No. 4 is neutral to operating and rate of replacement of structure decisions but is a disincentive to remodeling and new construction. It discriminates in favor of both deferred and noncommercial land uses. It is neutral, however, between use and nonuse of existing housing. It could be applied to owner-occupied properties only by special provisions. For this and other reasons, the tax would be exceedingly difficult to administer. Its yield would be cyclically much less stable than that of tax No. 2 and might prove inadequate in a severe depression. It is unobjectionable on grounds of equity, but the probable administrative difficulties are alone severe enough to rule it out as an alternative to tax No. 2.

Tax No. 5, the British "rates," has essentially the same qualities as tax No. 3 and hence cannot be considered an improvement over the present American system.

The characteristics of tax No. 6, an abatement, depend upon the basic tax with which it is combined. Assume for simplicity that it were to be combined with tax No. 2. Assume, as before, that it applies only to the *additional* values created by improved operation, condition of structure, remodeling or new construction, i.e., that it preserves the previously existing tax base. Then the extent of its resource-allocating effects obviously depends upon the length of the abatement period. It would be neutral to operating decisions as long as the abatement is allowed for improved operation. It would be neutral to remodeling decisions only if the allowed abatement were at least as long as the expected life of a rehabilitated building. Otherwise, it would reduce but not remove the disincentive to remodeling. It cannot be neutral to new-construction decisions (even if applicable to them), since it does not forgive the whole tax on improvements, but it would reduce the disincentive to new construction. Whether an abatement would be extended to owner-occupied housing on the same terms as to rental housing would depend on a political decision. An abatement program is certainly administratively feasible but would probably be somewhat more difficult to administer than tax No. 2. Its initial effect would probably be to reduce revenue yield below what it would otherwise have been; its long-run effect on yield is uncertain. It would discriminate inequitably between qualifying and nonqualifying property owners and might help middle-income tenants sooner than poor ones. Yet tax No. 6 is an attractive alternative. Its three drawbacks—possible administrative difficulty, possible loss of revenue, and inequity—are none of them decisive.

The effects of tax No. 7, a tax penalty, on quality of operation may range from the intended positive, through neutral, all the way down to an unintended negative result. Its effects on rate of replacement and remodeling are uncertain. It is unlikely to be applied to owner-occupied housing. It would add distinct administrative burdens to those of a basic tax. It might very slightly increase revenue. Unlike tax No. 6, it would not encourage adaptation of the existing stock of housing to changing demand conditions. It has possible merit as a supplement to a housing code, which suggests that it deserves consideration in connection with code reform rather than tax reform.

Conclusions and Recommendations

We have analyzed and compared alternative real estate taxes in the hope of finding one that would be more favorable than is the present American tax to quality of operation and rehabilitation of urban rental housing while at the same time not inferior to it on other grounds. We conclude that only tax No. 6 and, with certain qualifications, tax No. 1 are preferable to tax No. 2 on the criteria selected.

We have argued that shifting to tax No. 1 would narrow the real estate tax base too much in view of present revenue needs and would be inequitable to landowners unless untaxing buildings greatly increases the rent of land gross of tax. The threat to revenue could, however, be eliminated and the inequity much reduced by relying on a heavier land tax without altogether giving up the levy on improvements. Pittsburgh's "graded tax plan," described in Chapter 9, is just such an arrangement. It took effect over a period of ten years, during which the rate on buildings was, on a prearranged schedule, gradually lowered and that on land gradually raised until the goal was reached of a building rate set at only half the land rate. Such a plan protects revenue while reducing the disincentive effects of a tax on improvements. It hurts landowners but hurts them less than would a complete switch to tax No. 1. The Pittsburgh plan, or something like it, is therefore one of the preferred alternatives to the traditional American tax.

Tax No. 6, combined with the present American tax, is a second preferred alternative. It would probably be the easiest alternative to enact, first, because it appears superficially to help many people while hurting none (its inequity to owners of existing nonqualifying housing not being readily apparent), second, because it appears to cost nothing in revenue (the possible loss being of potential rather than actual tax receipts). Like the graded tax plan, it has successful precedents.

A third alternative combines elements of tax No. 1 and tax No. 6. This plan would (1) set a ceiling on building tax rates at their present level, (2) leave site-value rates free to rise as necessary in the future, and (3) allow taxes to be abated on any additional values created by new construction, rehabilitation, or improved quality of operation. Like tax No. 6, this combined scheme would probably be easier to enact than the Pittsburgh graded tax.

Which of the three plans would in the long run most stimulate new construction, remodeling, and improved quality of operation depends obviously on the initial tax rates and on how far the building rate can be reduced in the case of the Pittsburgh plan or how long it is abated in the two others. It is perhaps safe to say that either abatement scheme would have a greater immediate effect than the Pittsburgh plan, since an abatement can be granted all at once, while the Pittsburgh approach involves a gradual reduction. On the other hand, the Pittsburgh plan, once fully in effect, seems more likely to endure (as it has in Pittsburgh) than does an abatement program, which has about it more the air of temporary emergency legislation.

It is important to emphasize that our canvass of possible reforms has been deliberately limited to those alternatives that fall within the family of real estate taxes. More radical, and perhaps more desirable reforms of the real estate tax are conceivable if, as part of the reform program, one calls for additional revenue from taxes or charges outside the group included here. Along those lines, Dick Netzer's proposals certainly deserve very careful consideration.[41]

Major problems are not resolved by minor policy prescriptions; the means must be on the scale of the social forces they are designed to reshape. Seen in that perspective, none of the proposals made here can be considered radical. On the contrary, they would make only a modest contribution toward solving what is traditionally called "the housing problem." But there has been a disproportion in our thinking about housing and, more generally, about urban reconstruction: considering the heavy, continuous, and unyielding pressure of real estate taxes upon urban life, we have given far too little thought to the possible utility of real estate tax reform.

[41] See his *Economics of the Property Tax* (Washington, D. C., The Brookings Institution, 1966), Chap. VIII.

APPENDIX A

VACANCY RATES IN URBAN HOUSING

That overall vacancy rates were relatively high in the United States during the 1930s can be amply demonstrated; that there was a plentiful supply of vacant urban rental housing in the low-rent brackets is less easily shown on account of the paucity of data. One series that measures vacancies of the latter kind was developed by Leo Grebler.[1] His study deals with Manhattan's Lower East Side, unquestionably a slum area. From a variety of sources, Grebler compiled a series on vacancies for selected dates, which we present in part in Table A.1.

Included in Lower East Side vacancies were a substantial number of boarded-up units. Grebler points out that these accounted for an estimated 3.2 percent of the inventory in 1934, 5.8 percent in 1940, and over 2 percent in 1949.[2] Either way, the Lower East Side vacancy rate was high during the 1930s. It cannot be assumed without further study that equally high rates prevailed in other slum areas, since this one had long been declining. Nothing in the literature suggests, however, that slum vacancies were not ample in the typical city during the prewar decade.

In Table A.2 we present data for cities in all parts of the United States which show how tight the urban housing market became immediately after World War II, by comparison with

[1] *Housing Market Behavior in a Declining Area* (New York, Columbia University Press, 1952).

[2] *Ibid.*, p. 41. The estimating process used to take account of boarded-up units is described by Grebler in his Appendix D, pp. 173–80.

the prewar situation. Unlike Grebler's data, these cover ownership as well as rental units.

Grebler's data for Manhattan and the Lower East Side,
shown in Table A.1., illustrate a like trend. For both of those
areas, if the vacancies in boarded-up structures are omitted,
the vacancy rates from 1947 through 1949 are reduced to less
than 0.5 percent.

TABLE A.1

*Estimated Vacancy Rates in New York City,
Multi-Family Structures*

Date	Lower East Side	Manhattan	New York City
	(percent of total inventory of multi-family units)		
December, 1931	22.0	15.0	n.a.
February–May, 1934	23.8	18.6	13.7
January, 1939	15.5	11.3	n.a.
January, 1940	18.9	11.4	8.1
January, 1944	30.0	19.1	n.a.
March, 1947	3.4	3.2	n.a.
March, 1949	2.3	2.4	n.a.

Source: Leo Grebler, *Housing Market Behavior in a Declining Area* (New
York, Columbia University Press, 1952), Table 5, p. 38.

TABLE A.2

*Prewar vs. Postwar Vacancy Rates in Selected Cities
and Metropolitan Areas*

	Habitable Vacant Dwelling Units	
	(percent of total dwelling units)	
Area	April, 1940	Last 6 Months 1946
Los Angeles area	7.1	1.0
San Francisco city	7.3	1.0
Denver area	4.2	0.8
Chicago city	4.0	0.7
Detroit area	3.4	0.5
Boston city	6.7	1.1
New York City area	7.6	0.9
Houston area	5.2	1.5

Source: Housing and Home Finance Agency, *Housing Statistics Handbook*
(Washington D.C., 1948), Table 55, pp. 68–71 (cities selected by the author to
show wide geographic distribution).

APPENDIX B

STATISTICS
FOR MEASURING
STABILITY OF YIELD OF
ALTERNATIVE
REAL ESTATE TAXES

In order to make comparisons of the probable revenue characteristics of various alternative real estate taxes, it would be
desirable to have either a set of national or of local time series
for real estate covering gross rent receipts, net income, assessed
value of land and of improvements, tax payments, and so forth.
Unfortunately, these ideal data from which we could make a
consistent set of comparisons are not available: we have therefore pieced out the job with a combination of national, local,
and case-study statistics.

To measure the stability of tax No. 1 on assessed site value
and tax No. 2 on combined assessed value of site and
improvements we have used New York City data from Table B.1.

To estimate the probable stability of tax No. 3 on gross rent,
we have two series: a "U.S. Total" series based on Commerce
Department data and a "New York City Sample" series developed by Leo Grebler, both presented in Table B.2.

The Commerce Department gross-rent data were developed

in connection with the national income accounts, one component of which is net rental income of persons. The first column of Table B.2 is the sum of the following components of the Commerce Department data: (1) gross space rent paid for rental housing, (2) imputed gross space rent of owner-occupied homes, (3) total rent paid on farm property, and (4) total rent paid on nonfarm businesses.

The sum of these four components is not a complete account of the gross rent of real property, since it omits the imputed rental value of owner-occupied business and farm property. It is, however, the most inclusive national figure available. In column 2 of Table B.2 the column 1 data are converted to an index series (1929 = 100).

The Grebler series is an index of gross rent for a sample of 581 New York City properties.

To estimate the cyclical stability of tax No. 4 on real estate net income, we have two series from the same sources as, but not strictly comparable to, our two gross-rent series. These are presented in Table B.3.

The Commerce Department has published net-rent data for the same four categories which composed our gross-rent series. Their net rents are, however, net of real estate taxes, whereas we require net rent before taxes. Unfortunately, the annual amount of taxes was published only for the categories of rental housing and owner-occupied homes. Therefore, we could not correct farm or business net rent by adding back in the annual amount of taxes. Rather than attempt to estimate a correction for taxes, we omitted both the farm and the business rent components. Hence, net income in Table B.3 covers only rental and owner-occupied housing. Net income was derived by deducting all expenses except taxes (i.e., maintenance and repair, interest, depreciation, insurance, and miscellaneous) from the appropriate gross-rent data.

Grebler's "net-income" series is, as he points out, more properly labeled "net operating income." It consists of income remaining after deduction of all operating expenses and real estate taxes but before deduction of depreciation, debt charges, or federal and state income tax. On this definition the series fails to meet our requirements, and since the annual data Grebler published consist entirely of index numbers, there is no way of adjusting the net-income data to a more satisfactory basis. Grebler also published, however, a set of operating ratios for five-year average periods. Included among them are the ratio of net income to gross income and also the ratio of real estate taxes to gross income. Adding the two ratios yields a net-income figure that differs from the desired one only in including depreciation and debt charges, but this is the best that can be done with the given data. Combining the ratios as indicated, we find that net income before taxes, depreciation, or debt charges amounted to 73 percent of gross income in 1925–29, 67 percent in 1930–34, 60 percent in 1935–39, and 57 percent in 1940–44. Since we have an index of the movement of gross income over the period, we can obtain by multiplication an estimate of the movement of net income before taxes or depreciation. We present this as an index series, 1925–29 = 100, in Table B.3. The results obtained using the product of the five-year averages may differ somewhat from those that would be obtained by averaging the yearly products.

Appendix B

TABLE B.1

Assessed Value of Taxable Real Estate
in New York City

Year	Land ($ billions)	Total ($ billions)
1920	4.7	8.6
1921	5.0	10.0
1922	5.1	10.3
1923	5.2	10.6
1924	5.4	11.1
1925	5.7	11.0
1926	6.2	13.0
1927	7.1	14.5
1928	7.7	15.8
1929	8.2	17.1
1930	8.9	18.2
1931	9.2	18.8
1932	9.2	19.6
1933	8.8	18.4
1934	8.0	17.1
1935	7.7	16.7
1936	7.4	16.7
1937	7.6	16.6
1938	7.4	16.7
1939–40	7.4	16.6
1940–41	7.2	16.6
1941–42	7.0	16.2
1942–43	6.9	16.1
1943–44	6.8	16.0
1944–45	6.6	15.8
1945–46	6.6	15.9
1946–47	6.6	15.9
1947–48	6.8	16.9
1948–49	6.9	17.6
1949–50	7.0	18.1
1950–51	7.0	18.4
1951–52	7.0	18.8
1952–53	7.1	19.4
1953–54	7.1	19.8
1954–55	7.1	20.3
1955–56	7.2	21.0
1956–57	7.2	21.4
1957–58	7.3	21.9
1958–59	7.3	22.4
1959–60	7.8	23.5
1960–61	8.1	24.9

Source: City of New York, Annual Report of the Tax Commission and the Tax Department, various years.

TABLE B.2

Gross Rent of Real Estate

	U.S. Total		N.Y.C. Sample
Year	$ billions	Index (1929 = 100)	(1947–49 = 100)
1920	. . .	. . .	91
1921	. . .	. . .	102
1922	. . .	. . .	106
1923	. . .	. . .	109
1924	. . .	. . .	111
1925	. . .	. . .	113
1926	. . .	. . .	118
1927	. . .	. . .	120
1928	. . .	. . .	121
1929	16.5	100	124
1930	15.4	94	122
1931	13.9	84	117
1932	12.0	72	100
1933	10.6	64	82
1934	10.6	64	77
1935	10.9	66	75
1936	11.3	68	77
1937	11.9	72	80
1938	12.1	73	80
1939	12.5	76	78
1940	12.9	78	77
1941	14.1	85	76
1942	15.4	93	75
1943	16.2	98	77
1944	16.7	101	81
1945	17.2	104	86
1946	19.4	117	90
1947	21.7	131	94
1948	24.2	146	102
1949	25.9	157	104
1950	28.5	172	107
1951	31.2	189	. . .

Sources:

U.S. Total: H. D. Osborne, "Rental Income and Outlay—in the United States, 1929–52," *Survey of Current Business,* June, 1953, pp. 17–24.

New York City Sample: Leo Grebler, *Experience in Urban Real Estate Investment* (New York, Columbia University Press, 1955), Table 39, pp. 226–27. The Table 39 entry for 1938 reads "70" which is apparently a misprint for "80," since the subindex for residential cases rose 2 points from 1937 to 1938, while that for nonresidential cases fell 2 points, indicating the probability that the total index recorded no change.

Appendix B

TABLE B.3

Net Income of Real Estate

	Net Income from Housing, U.S. Total			Net Income of N.Y.C. Sample, Residential and Nonresidential	
Year	$ billions	Index (1929 = 100)		Years	Index (1925–29 = 100)
1929	5.38	100		1920–24	85
1930	5.01	93		1925–29	100
1931	4.48	83		1930–34	77
1932	3.66	68		1935–39	52
1933	2.78	52		1940–44	51
1934	2.42	45		1945–49	59
1935	2.43	45		1950	64
1936	2.58	48			
1937	2.94	55			
1938	3.42	64			
1939	3.51	65			
1940	3.62	67			
1941	4.02	75			
1942	4.76	88			
1943	5.26	98			
1944	5.68	106			
1945	5.86	109			
1946	5.83	108			
1947	6.05	112			
1948	6.98	130			
1949	8.26	154			
1950	9.14	170			
1951	10.06	187			
1952	11.33	211			

Sources:

Net income from housing, U.S. total: H. D. Osborne, "Rental Income and Outlay—in the United States, 1929–51," *Survey of Current Business,* June, 1953, pp. 17–24.

Net income of N.Y.C. sample: derived by the author from Leo Grebler, *Experience in Urban Real Estate Investment* (New York, Columbia University Press, 1955), Tables 39 and 59.

STATISTICS FOR TESTING THE ADEQUACY OF SITE VALUE AS A TAX BASE

In Chapter 10 a procedure is described for testing statistically whether a site-value tax can yield as much revenue as does the traditional American levy at current tax rates. In order to make the test, we require estimates of four statistics: (1) the capital value of land after capitalization of the present land tax, (2) the capital value of improvements after capitalization or shifting of the present building tax, (3) the effective rate of the present real estate tax (i.e., the ratio of tax revenue to full market value), and (4) the rate of interest for capitalization of the rent of land. The test then requires a calculation of the ratio of building value to land value and of the ratio of interest rate for capitalization to effective tax rate. A site-value tax can provide the required revenue only if the latter ratio exceeds the former.

Our estimate of the rate of interest for capitalization of land rent is described in Chapter 10. This Appendix describes the derivation of the other three required statistics both for the United States and for New York City.

For the United States as a whole we have data for 1956 compiled by the Census Bureau and data for the same year derived from figures in Raymond Goldsmith's *The National Wealth of the United States in the Postwar Period*. (See Table

C.1.) From the Goldsmith data on national wealth we can obtain an estimate of the value of buildings and the value of land, and hence of the ratio between them.[1] Since we are interested only in the ratio of buildings to land taxable under the conventional American real estate tax, we have extracted from his study sets of figures that exclude forest land, institutional land and buildings, and federal, state, and local government land and buildings. This leaves us with total values for private, noninstitutional land and buildings. For the year 1956 the ratio of the building total to the land total was 2.9:1. Since this study is concerned only with urban real estate, one would like to be able to refine the data further to exclude all rural land and buildings. As the data do not permit such an exclusion, the best that can be done is to remove farm land and buildings. That done, we arrive at a ratio of the value of private, noninstitutional, nonfarm buildings to land of 4.4:1 for 1956.

For the same year the Census Bureau, as part of the *1957 Census of Governments,* studied "Taxable Property Values in the United States" and obtained a figure for the aggregate assessed value of locally assessed taxable real property. The Census Bureau also investigated ratios of assessed value to market sales value for measurable sales during a six-month period. Applying these ratios to the assessed values, they obtained five different estimates of nationwide market value. These varied from $664.5 billion to $717.6 billion. We have chosen to work with the estimate of $689.9 billion, which falls nearest the middle of the range. It should be noted that all five estimates omit both the value of personal property and the value of property assessed by state agencies for local tax liability.

The values assessed during 1956 formed the base for taxes collected in 1957. Applying the Census Bureau figure for local

---

[1] Princeton, N.J., Princeton University Press, 1962. It should be noted that Goldsmith arrived at estimates of land value for some subgroups by applying structure-to-land ratios estimated in various ways to carefully developed series on structure value. Thus, the overall structure-to-land ratio we have derived from his study is not a ratio between two independently derived series. It is to some extent only a weighted average of the structure-to-land ratios with which he was working.

property tax revenue in 1957 to the 1956 value base would yield an estimate of the 1956 effective tax rate of 1.8 percent. This estimate is, however, somewhat too high because the revenue figure in the numerator includes tax revenue from personal property and property assessed by state agencies for liability to the local general property tax, while the value figure in the denominator excludes both. In order to avoid overestimating the effective tax rate, we can make a rough adjustment for this deficiency. Although the Census Bureau did not estimate the *market sales value* of the two classes of property mentioned above, it did publish data on their *assessed* value. In 1956, state-assessed property and locally assessed personal property accounted for 25.6 percent of the assessed value of property subject to the local general property tax.[2] If we reduce the 1957 tax revenue by that proportion, we obtain an effective tax rate of 1.3 percent on real property. This figure probably errs on the low side, since personal property (17.4 points of the 25.6 point adjustment) is usually taxed at rates far below those on real property. The true rate probably falls, therefore, between 1.3 and 1.8 percent on the basis of Census data.

Alternatively, we can calculate the effective rate using the data derived from Goldsmith on taxable values as the denominator and the Census Bureau tax revenue figure as the numerator. This procedure yields an effective tax rate of 1.6 percent in 1956. Again, the estimate is somewhat too high on account of the inclusion of personal property tax revenue in the numerator. This result, together with the calculation from Census data, points to an effective tax rate of about 1.5 percent, which we use for the value *t*, in Chapter 10.

Data for testing the adequacy of New York City site values as a tax base are presented in Table C.2 and are self-explanatory except for the adjustment used to derive the effective tax rate (line 7) from the apparent tax rate (line 6). At issue here is the question, how accurately did assessments reflect market values in 1960–61? Assessments are known to lag behind market values when the latter are rising, as they have been since World War II. Haig and Shoup found the citywide assessment-to-

2 *1957 Census of Governments*, Vol. V, Table 2, p. 23.

TABLE C.1

*Data for Measuring Adequacy of Land Value
as a Tax Base, U.S. Totals*

Line No.		1956 (Except as Noted)
	Census Bureau Data	
1	Market value of locally assessed U.S. real estate	$689.9 billion
2	Local general property tax revenue (1957)	$12.231 billion
3	Local general property tax revenue reduced 25.6%	$9.100 billion
4	Ratio of Line 2 to Line 1 (effective tax rate)	0.018
5	Ratio of Line 3 to Line 1 (effective tax rate)	0.013
	Goldsmith Data	
6	Value of private, noninstitutional structures	$562.97 billion
7	Value of private, noninstitutional, nonforest land	$194.29 billion
8	Ratio of Line 6 to Line 7	2.9:1
9	Line 6 less farm structures	$528.60 billion
10	Line 7 less farm land	$120.33 billion
11	Ratio of Line 9 to Line 10	4.4:1
12	Sum of Lines 6 and 7	$757.26 billion
13	Ratio of Line 2 to Line 12 (effective tax rate)	0.016

Sources:
Line 1: *1957 Census of Governments*, Vol. V, Table 12, p. 81.
Line 2: *Ibid.*, Vol. V, Table 1, p. 21.
Line 3: *Ibid.*, Vol. V, Table 2, p. 23, for the 25.6 percent factor.
Lines 6 and 9: Raymond W. Goldsmith, *The National Wealth of the United States in the Postwar Period* (Princeton, N.J., Princeton University Press, 1962), Tables A-35 and A-36.
Lines 7 and 10: *Ibid.*, Tables A-40, A-41, and A-42.

TABLE C.2

Data for Measuring Adequacy of Land Value
as a Tax Base, New York City

Line No.		1960–61 (Fiscal Year)
1	Assessed value of taxable buildings ª	$15,773.9 million
2	Assessed value of taxable land ª	$ 8,131.8 million
3	Ratio of line 1 to line 2	1.94:1
4	Sum of lines 1 and 2	$23,905.7 million
5	Tax levy ª	$ 1,014.7 million
6	Ratio of line 5 to line 4 (apparent tax rate)	0.0424
7	Line 6 reduced by 25% (estimated effective tax rate)	0.0318

ª Franchise values and tax payments on same omitted. Public utility corporation values and tax payments included.

Sources:

Line 1: The City of New York, *Annual Report of the Tax Commission as of June 30, 1960*, pp. 38, 39, and 40.

Line 2: *Ibid.*, pp. 38 and 39.

Line 5: The City of New York, *Annual Report of the Comptroller for the Fiscal Year 1960–61*, pp. 14 and 17.

sales-price ratio in 1950 to be 0.87.[3] In all probability the ratio has declined further since then. The *1957 Census of Governments* provides only some indirect clues: it includes state-by-state but, for obvious political reasons, not city-by-city assessment-sales ratios. The New York State ratio for all properties was 52.8 percent. For New York City it must have been very much higher, since the state figure is pulled down by the low ratios for farm property and acreage (27.9 percent) and for single-family houses. The statewide ratios relevant for the city were: residential property, 49.4 percent; commercial and industrial property, 78.2 percent; and vacant lots, 40.9 percent.[4] In each category the ratios were still higher for properties of above average value, which are precisely the classes that dominate aggregate value in New York City. From these clues one may hazard the guess that assessment-sales ratios in the City may have fallen to about 75 percent by 1960–61. Therefore, the effective tax rate would be 75 percent of the apparent rate.

[3] Robert M. Haig and Carl S. Shoup, *The Financial Problem of the City of New York* (New York, June, 1952), pp. 134-35.

[4] *1957 Census of Governments*, Vol. V, Table II, Part B, p. 62.

INDEX